The
GREAT AMERICAN
Wise Ass Poetry
Anthology

The GREAT AMERICAN Wise Ass Poetry Anthology

edited by

Jerry Bradley
Ulf Kirchdorfer

LITERARY PRESS
LAMAR UNIVERSITY

ISBN: 978-1-942956-15-0
Library of Congress Control Number: 2015959093
Manufactured in the United States

Cover painting: Albert Bierstadt, "Old Faithful," 1881

Lamar University Literary Press
Beaumont, Texas

For

Barbara Lee Bradley (1944-2015)

Bjorn Kirchdorfer

Poetry from Lamar University Literary Press

Charles Behlen, *Failing Heaven*
Alan Berecka, *With Our Baggage*
David Bowles, *Flower, Song, Dance: Aztec and Mayan Poetry*
Jerry Bradley, *Crownfeathers and Effigies*
Matthew Brennan, *One Life*
Paul Christensen, *The Jack of Diamonds is a Hard Card to Play*
Chip Dameron, *Waiting for an Etcher*
William Virgil Davis, *The Bones Poems*
Jeffrey DeLotto, *Voices Writ in Sand*
Mimi Ferebee, *Wildfires and Atmospheric Memories*
Larry Griffin, *Cedar Plums*
Ken Hada, *Margaritas and Redfish*
Michelle Hartman, *Disenchanted and Disgruntled*
Michelle Hartman, *Irony and Irreverence*
Katherine Hoerth, *Goddess Wears Cowboy Boots*
Lynn Hoggard, *Motherland*
Gretchen Johnson, *A Trip Through Downer, Minnesota*
Ulf Kirchdorfer, *Chewing Green Leaves*
Janet McCann, *The Crone at the Casino*
Erin Murphy, *Ancilla*
Laurence Musgrove, *Local Bird*
Dave Oliphant, *The Pilgrimage, Selected Poems: 1962-2012*
Kornelijus Platelis, *Solitary Architectures*
Carol Coffee Reposa, *Underground Musicians*
Jan Seale, *The Parkinson Poems*
Carol Smallwood, *Water, Earth, Air, Fire, and Picket Fences*
Glen Sorestad *Hazards of Eden*
W.K. Stratton, *Ranchero Ford/ Dying in Red Dirt Country*
Wally Swist, *Invocation*
Jonas Zdanys (ed.), *Pushing the Envelope, Epistolary Poems*

For information on these and other Lamar Universit Literary Press books go to

www.lamar.edu/literarypress

CONTENTS

Introduction

It would be beautifully disingenuous to say that the idea for *The Great American Wise Ass Poetry Anthology* came to us "at a cocktail party after the dangerous third martini," to borrow Graham Greene's words about reviewing films. First of all, neither of us is an aficionado of martinis, as the word "aficionado" bumped ahead of martinis should indicate. We also don't like cocktail parties, so-called events which denote a sense of entitlement of participants that includes the unpleasant strangulation of males by necktie and the confinement of women in pantyhose. (*The Wall Street Journal* says this garment is making a comeback). These types of events are best experienced vicariously by watching any number of series on PBS, among them *Downton Abbey*, which at first seem very refreshing, like a beer or margarita on a hot day.

The idea for *The Great American Wise Ass Poetry Anthology* came to us like champagne corks popped by dorks who couldn't stop the over-flowing poetic elixir on a day we were both stone sober, conducting institutional business for our academies, feeling much like pinups for Theodore Roethke's "Dolor." Add to Roethke's sad pencils any number of 21st-century committees and technological malfunctions, and poor Ted would have been driven mad and fled onto the tennis court or gone horseback riding with his student Jane. We retreated forward to the wise ass poetry sanatorium.

If *The Great American Wise Ass Poetry Anthology* is a reactionary move, it is a volley for which we make no apologies. People who play checkers don't apologize, and neither do people who play chess, though maybe the second group should. Either way, the racket of a world we live in appears all too frequently at best a mild hangover, a blur, or a smog of people parroting established scenarios, minus the colorful plumage. But when beaks cross, feathers may get ruffled or even fly before peace is restored to the aviary.

Poets find various ways to capture and escape everyday life, and their work receives myriad labels and is sorted into all sorts of schools and movements. Such pedantic information can be found in various anthologies from which those of us who work in an educational capacity lead our students to drink. But anyone of integrity—and what used to be called common sense—who dips into one of them may need to come up for air as he or she wonders why there is so little in those myopia-conducive collections that does not deal with killing oneself, suffering until death, or losing out on the American Dream (either prematurely or post-ecstasy). Add any scenarios you like (but don't like), and you are left with little redemption and may on a good day feel ready to audition for the part of E. A. Robinson's Eben Flood. And while you're away from the town below, be sure to recognize how few expressions of positive emotion contemporary poetry publications offer. We don't mean the kind that rhymes on brightly-colored greeting cards but serious poetry that chronicles a reality as valid as Sylvia Plath's. If you are visualizing Plath in a handstand, you are heading in the right direction. Yes, we are heading in the direction of wise ass poetry. How do you like your apples now, Mr. Frost?

The antidote wise ass poetry offers is not an escape from emotion (with no apologies whatsoever to "Tough Shit" Eliot, as one of us heard a Brit with a working-class accent refer to the man from St. Louis over burgers and beer in Houston), but an escape from emotion that presents on one end the extremes of death and despair and on the other mindless happy-happy-happiness.

Enter the wise ass poet and the editors attempting to finger the pulse of the like-minded. Our call for submissions provided the following definition and directions:

> *Variations on "wise ass" listed by the Urban Dictionary include "smartass, dumbass, chickenshit, smart aleck, smartypants," and* more potent expressions not listed here. We are looking for excellent poems that just happen to be snarky, irreverent, impudent, subversive, *smart ass, etc. — no doggerel. Any parodies or satires should be biting rather than polite (unless the politeness is part of the subversion).*

And, of course, all must be funny—whatever that means. We must be amused!

"Smart ass" was somewhere in our minds as we shouted across the technological canyons of our vast land, but we hoped "wise ass" would add an aura of politeness. We thought that if we used corn on our hook instead of stink bait, we might attract trout as well as catfish. We charged no submission fee and offered cash awards to the best poems. We waited for poetic revelations from the proverbial church lady like the second coming of Christ; then we began to see some wise ass headers in our email inboxes, then a steady rain, and, holy shit, Noah, the flood of nearly eight hundred submissions was upon us.

While we know plenty of wise asses and know for sure there are many wise ass poets, we are not funded by a grant from any institution and its watchful staff (as in a "mental retreat"), and, as wise asses ourselves, we thought it proper to read every one of the poems personally. We could not bring ourselves to farm out the poems to other readers, no matter how enjoyable the task might sometimes be, the *petit mort* of many literary magazines.

What makes a wise ass poem we leave to the readers and critics in hope that Robert Graves's line, "The thundering text, the snivelling commentary" from his delightful "Of Ogres and Pygmies," is not the result of our endeavor. His poem actually offers a good example of what a wise ass poem can be: excellent poetic execution with a punch line, an admonishment that we not take ourselves too seriously or believe we are gods of poetry, though we speak the truth nevertheless. "Of Ogres and Pygmies" touches on the affliction of poetry, the poet-patient forced into bed rest, afraid of taking risks for fear of fracture or escalating other negative symptoms, too aware of the critic as audience. In this kind of situation, the poet usually takes no chances and does not go in for the kill. Unfortunately, the first scenario is most prevalent when one considers the competent but safe *dreck* that gets published these days and has been for many years. A wise ass poet risks alienating the literary establishment, the gatekeepers of publication. We can say with certainty that James Dickey, for example, paid a steep price for publishing what some would consider a wise ass poem, "The Sheep-Child." The poem once was included in the *Norton Anthology* but no longer is because someone does not consider a subversive poem about bestiality to be worthy of literary publication. Is there no room in the world of poetry for "Squeal like a pig!"? That world is worse off for the absence—unless you are Ned Beatty's fictitious Bobby.

Wise ass poetry does not have to be outright provocative, nor does it have to be angry. It does not even have to be clever. Whatever the conditions of its origin, wise ass poetry can be terrible or wonderful; it can be sad, happy, mournful, muted, or whatever mood one obtains from reading the poem. But wise ass poetry is subversive and, make what you will of the word, it is a delicious combination of *sub* (under) and *versus*.

It is customary in introductions to anthologies and collections by several authors to dutifully mention some of the works and summarize them so that the reader will want to feed more quarters into the machine. But such introductions may induce readers to rely on someone else's formulations rather than consider the poems. We encourage readers of this volume to instead take a turn dancing, feeling, touching, or hearing—whatever you do in the privacy of your own with the poem is your business—each poem, in no particular order. In the spirit of readership and a somewhat Whitmanesque embrace and sampler, we will tango only briefly across the surface of the dance floor with some poems in our introduction only to send you off in your own direction to do your own thing.

That these wise ass poets know their craft will be obvious: their quatrains and villanelles can turn on a dime. Tradition lingers in their work, and you can hear Shakespeare, Frost, Rilke, Dickinson, and others in their footsteps. Some of us no doubt remember from our early days a wise ass comment as we sat in school benches where some wag piped up about what the teacher was bent on force feeding, a remark that elicited a chuckle, a laugh, or (depending on the age group), a good beating from the teacher. Just what is a good beating? The kind where a boy has his head tapped while dancing with his brutish father.

With and despite our education, we can't always know whether the author of the wise ass poem before us really means exactly what he or she says (with no apologies to Eliot again), but we can be certain that whatever is laid out before us on the page, however filtered or masked, presents a force from someone who does not readily buy into or accept the status quo or the plans made by those who rule, life's begrudging legislators. The wise ass poet holds his own court and exerts whatever influence he or she has on the page, both animated and frozen at the same time.

These are the poets who have drunk too much poetry, who know its expectations and find wisdom in the drink. But they are not necessarily postmodernists. They are believers (but not believers in bullshit) who ultimately live in two worlds. In one they acknowledge that bumping one's knee into a table hurts and is not merely a linguistic construct. But in the other they recognize how lovely it is to behold the banquet laid out on the table. When the frame of the painting becomes visible, it is time to go back to work, the real kind that puts food on the table and satisfies a basic need. A wise poet may live in a garret, but he or she would not be ashamed of living in a beach condo.

Realizing that in order to practice one's art one must hold down a day job, the wise ass poet is (for the most part) gainfully and practically employed. However, the poet may still dream that old Uncle Gold Testicles will die suddenly and bequeath a huge inheritance that will free the poet to go forth and multiply his or her art on a massive scale.

This is to say, as this introduction has done, that there is some great wise ass poetry out there, often not given the opportunity to be voiced or published, often unappreciated. But God and the Devil know that wise ass poetry will rise. And if for some reason courses are taught in wise ass poetry all across the country, so be it. We are sure some/all of us will all have something wise ass but poetic to say about it.

Jerry Bradley
Ulf Kirchdorfer

Fixing Fence
Michael Albright

Something there is that doesn't love a fence,
and it's called an all-terrain vehicle.
Who lets a five year old ride around
the backyard on one? My neighbor, that's who.
She says it's ok, it's designed for his age,
but I say, this is crazy, but, just look at her.
I'd never call a person stupid, and, I guess
there's no way to prove a thing will happen,
but some things seem more than predictable,
like a little boy driving a four-wheeler
through a fence. I really don't get it,
because I *know* these people watch a lot of TV.
What did they think would happen?
I'll bet at his birthday there will be
grandpa holding a piñata on a stick
awaiting the inevitable shot to the groin.
(Darla. Now there's a trailer park name
if I ever heard one. Not sure how they ended
up here—rumor is they won
two-hundred grand in the lottery—
my money's on a meth lab in the basement.)
Maybe she put him up to it,
taped him doing it, hoping
for the ten thousand dollar grand prize.
on *America's Funniest Videos*.
Thank God the kid wasn't hurt,
or I might be facing a lawsuit. After all,
if I hadn't put that fence there,
Damien couldn't have hit it. But he's the reason
I put it there in the first place.
(Yes, Damien, like the kid in *The Omen*,
but I don't think he's evil, just overlooked.)
He wouldn't stay out of our yard,
(which was not an issue before the pool—
then it became necessity). Even still,
a six-foot wooden fence couldn't stop him.
He's resourceful, determined, and brave.
When I pull into my the driveway
he's always waiting in his front yard
by the busy road that he shouldn't be near,
but his mom is nowhere in sight, never is.
He always yells *Hi, neighbor*, as I get out
(he never remembers my name). I say *hi* back.
What are you doing? he asks, always the same,
always the same answer. *Going in my house.*

Don't get me wrong, I don't hate the kid.
I know he's not getting any attention.
When Darla and I meet at the hole in the fence,
she tells me she doesn't think she's responsible—
(she looks flirty in her tube top and too short
jean-shorts, fraying and showing the half-moon
of her ass, and I try to ignore that voice
telling me she's sexy in a slutty kind of way)
if I hadn't built the fence with the posts and beams
facing out (so I wouldn't have to see them),
then he probably wouldn't have gone through.
She takes a long drag on her Salem. We both know
this is bullshit, but it doesn't matter—
she says doesn't have the money.
I wouldn't know it if she did. Luckily,
I can fix the damage with hammer and nails.
Back in therapy, they taught me a saying,
Everyone is doing the best that they can.
Well, maybe that's true, but sometimes,
the best just ain't good enough.
Keep the little bastard out of my yard.
Good fences make good neighbors, all right—
you stay on your side, and I'll stay on mine.

Kinzua Bridge State Park, 2003
Michael Albright

When I called you from the viaduct,
without a single soul in sight,
no other cars in the slushy lot,
no visitor's center open for spring,
no rangers or workmen or anyone,
just me, the squirrels, and a sheen of mud,
how amazed I was to have service here,
300 feet up this abandoned trestle,
the trickling middle of nowhere below—
when I said you'd never guess what I'd just done,
you, sister of brothers, mother of sons, said
You peed off that fucking bridge, didn't you?

Three months later a big wind came through
and left a twisted and tangled heap.
Some say phantom trains collided,
and the wailing of the ghosts of ghosts
skipped for miles in the boreal night,
as far as Cyclone and Shinglehouse.

The Art of Aging

Dorothy Alexander

At ninety, I'll wear a faded housedress and a clean starched apron just like Great Aunt Charity Polk did. I will carry a flyswatter with me at all times and smack at small children when they come too close. I'll slip away from my room at Rosewood Manor and wheel down to the corner tavern. I'll order a short beer, dip snuff from a little tin box and spit in the potted plants. I'll cuss whenever I damn well please, and talk on my cell phone as loud as I want. I'll tell the same story over and over with only slight changes and pretend I don't see people rolling their eyes. I will diagnose my doctor's lumbago and lecture him on its treatment. I will break wind wherever and whenever the urge strikes me, then glare at the nearest person and say, "If you don't mind!" In church I'll pull my hat low over my face and pretend to pray while I click my heels on the floor to annoy the Christians.

And when I die, it will be on a quiet Sunday afternoon just as everyone is settling down for a nap. That's the best damned time of day to raise a ruckus.

Cannibalized

Dorothy Alexander

First, they took my tonsils.

I howled pitifully
—until the ice cream came.

Not long afterwards, they
came for my appendix.

Then, they took a cyst here,
an unspecified growth there,
not to mention the teeth,
one at a time at odd moments.

I swear there were times
they had a clipboard
checklist, crossing off
each item as they took it.

Hundreds of little vials
of blood, ingrown toenails,
warts, moles, fatty tumors,
bits for biopsies, gall bladder.
The whole reproductive
apparatus went out the door.

I feel like an old Chevrolet
no engine, no wheels,
rusting in a junkyard,
behind a wood fence
plastered with hubcaps
and a sign that says
Beware the Dog.

If You Can . . .
Brian Allgar

If you can make her laugh, that's half the battle,
especially if she's married to a bore;
if, secretly, you think of girls as cattle,
yet treat her like a lady, not a whore;
if you can undo bra-straps single-handed
while murmuring enticements in her ear;
if you can make her think you're being candid
when telling her the lies she wants to hear;
if you, my friend, can easily persuade her
to sample things she's never tried before,
or if she sighs with pleasure when you've laid her,
and smiles as you sneak out by the back door;
if you can tolerate her endless prattle
(and never tell her "Darling, get a life"),
her gossip and her foolish tittle-tattle—
then you're the bastard who seduced my wife!

In Case You've Wondered
Fred Alsberg

That last time I knocked on your door
even your dog knew
you didn't love me no more.
When a gruff male voice upstairs yelled,
"She's not home,"
I turned and, walking away,
thought of the first time I saw you,
Do you recall? It was one morning at Phil's.
With everyone at the table your audience,
you waved your cigarette
to the rise and fall of that fluent musical voice of yours.
And like your favorite dog, I too gazed adoringly,
as you fingered the top button of your blouse,
then doused your cigarette
in a plate of spread yellow egg.
Yes, everything you do, you do with ease,
so when you asked me to move out
by the uh . . . end of the week,
my mind took a long slide on black ice—
You suggested I "get a U-Haul."
Within days, I was on my way
to make a barricade of boxes
in a friend's empty basement,
then leave for where palm trees
and the ocean would soothe me,
yet even seated in a beach chair, sipping a mojito,
I still held onto this one last hope:
that maybe . . .
someday . . .
with the stars perfectly aligned,
you would meet someone just like you.

Curtains

Lloyd Aquino

In my worst nightmare,
I'm the hero of the piece,
which means: nobly and stoically laying down my life
on the train tracks while some damsel yells "Distress!"
and runs me over for the next two reels.

(Because Joseph Campbell says every journey's
the same and sometimes that means evisceration)

So I'm comatose but wide awake
thanks to the sleep paralysis some hellspawn gave me,
ironically enough, in my sleep, and it was a momentary lapse,
a character flaw tragic enough to sell tickets.
I spend half the time saying "As you wish" over and again
with different inflections, or I invent new syllables,
              like "A-has you-uh a-wish,"
or I wink after two beats instead of thirteen.

(Because catchphrases and movie posters
are like fences and neighbors, is what the suits say,
and they're footing the bill and enabling my heroine addiction,
which finally gets resolved in Act Three
thanks to Aerosmithian power chords
and slow motion editing)

                        At the denouement,
the object of my affection inflicts special effects
to cause infection that spreads until the credits roll.

        Yes, there are outtakes.

                Yes, they'll be on the DVD.

        Yes, we're already planning the sequel.

                Yes, the commemorative cup is on sale
                in the lobby, half off with a box of Jujubes.

Next time, my nightmare will take place at sea,
and we'll reference the original ad nauseam
until the audience is nauseous with noxious laughter,
but next time work on channeling your pathos;
you'll need it to fit into the wardrobe.
That's what the director says
before he slaps me back to life, back to reality,

and I sit up and scream as my tongue gets caught
in the snap of the clapboard.

The last thing I hear is,
"Try a long 'a' instead of a short one
next time your mouth is bleeding,
and, for the love of Pete,
make those tears more believable."

Odds

Lloyd Aquino

Last night, a punk concert broke out at a poetry reading off Nogales.
According to the math, this happens one in seventeen times.
This time, the band played tributes to teen moms and circle jerks
(consecutively, not concurrently). A candy machine was involved.
This had never happened before in all of recorded history.

One in five poetry readings ends in multiple acts of hugging.

One in six ends in regret that has nothing to do with alcohol.

One in seven begins with someone losing their innocence.

One in two involves the song "Kumbaya."

Once every thousand poetry readings, a rapture happens,
and those of us left behind auction off jewelry, automobiles, the odd sex toy.
Someone always speaks too fast and someone else always overbids, usually
on the odd sex toy. The last rapture happened in Rancho Cucamonga,
and one lucky sinner got an ivory-handle switchblade for a buck-fifty
and an old condom.

One in twenty-five poetry readings will involve the loss of a limb.

Every other poetry reading, someone makes a drunken confession.
This usually has something to do with statutes of limitation or else
the real reason behind the self-portrait tattoo on one's, well, you know.

Every other poetry reading, a poet has a moment of clarity.
Half the time, it happens in the middle of a poem about casual sex,
the other half in the middle of a piece about that trip to Europe.
Nine times out of ten, the poet recalls some long-forgotten trauma.
The other time, the poet recalls reading Proust's *Remembrance of
        Things Past*.

One in three poetry readings occurs in the poet's natural habitat.
Imagine dim lights stuttering Bukowski in Morse code, uncomfortable
chairs, the smell of a microphone's frayed wiring and coffee beans.
Hand-woven scarves and horn-rimmed glasses are ubiquitous.

No poetry reading ever involves un-ironic finger-snapping.

One in four readings, someone un-ironically invokes Ginsberg's "Howl."

One in eleven, someone un-ironically invokes Neruda.

One in a million, someone un-ironically invokes the singer Jewel.

One in fifty poetry readings features a poet who loves himself
a little too much, with the resulting spectacle making all save one
in the audience a little too uncomfortable because public lewdness
is a near-universal taboo. He compliments himself after every piece
and gazes up at heaven wrapped in fluorescent lighting.
Three poems in, he's forgotten that anyone's there listening,
and two poems later, everyone else has gone to their happy place.

One in one-point-three-one-four poetry readings features a poet
who loathes everything he's ever written and is really only there
because self-flagellation means too much of a time commitment.

At every poetry reading, the compliments are always sincere.

On average, a poetry reading gives birth to eleven-point-seven new poems.
Ten-point-four of them are sometime thereafter read in front of an open
        mic,
rendering the mathematics of this poem hopelessly obsolete.

Memo

Barbara Astor

Under no circumstances will you be permitted to speak
directly to anyone. When someone calls, you are required
to let the line ring until it is answered by an intermediary.
If you have any questions regarding the message, do not
speak directly to anyone. An intermediary will intervene
if you do not return your keyed-in or recorded message
through the intermediary. Except when leaving recorded
messages through the intermediary, you will wear head-
phones at all times. You will not speak directly to anyone
who approaches you. An intermediary will intervene. At
home, you will not speak to anyone without an intermediary.
When you are not speaking to anyone anywhere through the
intermediary, you will wear headphones at all times. You
will talk continuously through an intermediary when driving.
At all times, you will be driving with one hand. Wherever you
roam, you will be driving with one hand across America
talking continuously until you stand in what's left of any open
field along the way and scream, but only through an intermediary.

Twin

Barbara Astor

We were treated as one
when it was convenient
and counted as two
for the same reason.

The order never changed
for baths before bedtime.
We were last, expected
to share the same tub water.
The cistern tank low,
the fights ensuing between us
over who would bathe first.

Bonds in each of our names
with like denominations.
Two for an older brother,
two for a younger sister.
And for us, one each.

Squabbling over yearbooks
to split the back pages
for high school classmates to sign,
and all the other myriad ways
for a middle class family
to save, to account for the duplicity
of unexpected twins.
All the ways to make us pay
for being so deceitful.

Tarzan Agonistes
Michael Baldwin

Picture Weissmuller's Tarzan swooping
thru the jungle on those conveniently
located liana vines,
his anthropoid, tonsilloid war yodel
echoing for miles around,
causing elephants to explode in wrath,
rhinos to rumble up dust,
lions to cringe in crazed terror,
tigers—(tigers in Africa?)—yes, tigers to tremble,
herds of zig-zagging zebras to stampede.
Then, he swings out over the crocodile-
infested pool and plunges in with a perfect
swan dive, swims like mad through
hoards of roaring hippos,
swarms of snapping crocs,
finally to the far shore where Jane
waits anxiously, her quivering bosoms
seeming at every moment about to escape
their meager confinement in that tiny,
but fashionable, leopard skin strapless.
He races toward her, hurls himself
upon the enormous python that,
unknown to her, had been about to engulf her.
He wrestles its writhing coils until
it is vanquished, then he embraces Jane,
holding her, trembling deliciously,
against the heaving of his mighty chest.
"Oh, thank you for saving me, Tarzan,
But the reason I sent the chimp to find you
was to ask: do you think my lizard sandals
or my zebra pumps go better with this dress?"

Eve Gives a Pep Talk

Melissa Balmain

Why obsess about negative stuff all the time—
how I got us in deep with my overhyped crime—
when, in plenty of ways, our disgrace is sublime?

To begin with, since God kicked us out with no pardon,
we haven't been getting those blisters that harden
if, six days a week, you've been pruning His garden.

Another great thing about not living there:
low humidity! None of that rainforest air!
From sunrise to sunset, we've both got good hair.

And be honest, what red-blooded pair wouldn't choose,
after paying their buck-naked, barefooted dues,
to wear some nice outfits and (OMG) shoes?

And who wouldn't like privacy? Certainly Eden
was perfect for walking or scattering seed in,
but, man, I felt watched when it came time for breedin'.

Best of all, there's the *food*. Our new diet's a beaut
(even though, I'll admit, it can make a gal toot).
Hello, lox and brisket; so long, boring fruit.

Aria da Capo
Carolyn Banks

to marriage

At first
she's pretty, she's fun.
He's sexy, he makes her laugh.
They make out, make love
and marry.

Soon
he doesn't want to go anywhere
or do anything,
even talk very much.
So she stops wearing makeup
and gets fat
and really snotty.

They get fatter and
more taciturn
until one of them
meets someone else
worth getting slim for,
worth talking to,
worth going places with.

At first.

The Magic Number

Walter Bargen

Do you know the strongest muscle, the tongue, is what I said, and won a CD, just by calling a radio station at six a.m. Third time this week I'm a winner and I don't even own a CD player. The powers of tongue could sell asteroids. A believer wants to plant the word of God on the moon in case we blow ourselves up. When I see those thick, limp, bovine appendages shrink-wrapped in meat coolers with not a bellow left in them, my faith is speechless.

Then I'd heard it takes more muscles to frown than to smile, and I won again—a large pizza supreme. At work I'm known as the muscular cynic. They can't tell the difference between a scowl and a frown. People ought to congratulate me for challenging myself so many hours each day—sticking my tongue out at hundreds of unsealed envelopes and not them. Asked how I'm doing, at my best I say, "It's going." Nobody asks where.

I win, I lose: Metallica, Judas Priest, Black Sabbath, axing out
tunes in little plastic boxes. I can't hear a deafening note. What I do hear is a son slamming his open palm against a wall so hard it shivers, scaring the cockroaches and the exterminator. All I said was I told you so. A daughter refuses and refuses, her chorus an industrial grade whining. My wife goes deeper and deeper. I sleep with this week's rumors. Most of the time I get a busy signal, or I'm the tenth caller when nine is the magic number.

Where Grass Is Greener

Walter Bargen

This morning, turning off the freeway,
driving under the overpass, I'm astonished to see
the embankment covered with concrete. Out of the construction
joints grow thin lines of knee-high grass, and I desire to be
that grass, to be out on the road where it grows
in solid spite of it all.

Standing in the hall at work,
brown tie clashing with blue pants, I describe this feeling
to four coworkers, who've never before wanted
to be knee-high grass.

I return to my cubicle and grab
the silver-pedestaled lipstick holder, a swathed cherub centered
on six cylindrical openings, that my daughter threw in the garbage,
that I brought to work to use as a pencil holder, and now hold
in front of me as a hood ornament. I step into the hall,
make loud engine noises—the grinding of gears, the squeal
of tires—race toward them, spin once on one foot,
make crashing sounds—the wrenching metal, the twisting
of bumpers, the rain of shattered glass—and then collapse
into the grass growing in the hallway.

from The Miniature Vedas
Tony Barnstone

A Failure

She says, "I think I *could*
be anorexic. I just don't have
the discipline.

*

A Grimm Tale

Once upon a time
she loved him. Then
she just fucking stopped.

*

"The Kalahari Kung

only have sex every five years,"
she said, "so don't tell me
you *need* sex."

*

Greek Ruins

Looking up through the streets of Athens
the boy cries, "Look!
You can see the Apocalypse!"

*

There's Something So Sad

about one shoe left by the roadside.
But underwear left at the beach,
that's just funny.

*

In His Dream He Sees an Ancient Japanese Knife,

and on it, written, DEATH.
Now that would be a hell
of a knife to cook with.

23

*

"One Good Thing about Divorce," She Said,

"I get to stop
being a character
in your damn poems."

My Girlfriend's Eyes Are Something Like the Sun
Tony Barnstone

My girlfriend's eyes are something like the sun,
Capable of incinerating ire.
Like distant drones her glances rain down fire
That roasts my heart until it feels well done.
Roses are all colors, but think "red."
That's how much rouge she cakes upon each cheek.
It's true she's like an animal in bed,
But in the morning, boy does her breath reek.
I love to hear her speak. Her voice trombones,
Trumpets, and tubas like a marching band.
I'm slightly deaf but feel it in my bones
And muscles turned to jelly, understand?
And though her eyes like bright coals make me bake,
I think my girlfriend's rare as bloody steak.

The Sermon on the Liquid Kitty

Tony Barnstone

Persuasive supple dancer blooming pretty
by the wet-bar with a nightshade sigh, you're
such a chiquita banana, such a Betty.
Please, bust this losing streak, show me the door
to your red heart or your blue bed. It's true
I'm just a bonehead, but even hair-shirt-
ers with thorn-whips and stakes need sex. And who
can really grasp how strange it is to flirt,
how queer we are to strangers? I have seen
them smoking in the streets outside of clubs
and perving at each other. I have seen
the tilted pink neon cocktail glass, pubs
whose patrons think, *knock boots, suck face, muff dive,*
and *boff.* They're thinking with the trouser snake,
the pecker, peter, boner, pud. They live
to get retarded, get stupid. They ache
to get inside your body. Yes, I know
I'm one of them. My life is on the fritz.
I can't think my way out of this one, so
I'm thinking, *whoopie, nookie, quickie, jizz.*

Birthday in Beijing

Joan E. Bauer

April thunderclouds in battleship formation
but the rain is light as we touch down.
At last, the swarming, noisy, candy-

colored streets of the city. Breakfast:
soy boiled eggs, red beans, dumplings,
strong coffee—four cups. For jet lag.

Tiananmen? Closed for 'renovation'
& no one is surprised. So our guide Mr. Ho
distracts us, talking about love, Beijing-style,

how young people pay $11 for a broadcast ad,
while old-timers ballroom dance in the park.
There are still arranged marriages. A groom

doesn't see the bride until the veil is lifted.
He tells us: *In China it's not rude to ask*
personal questions, even of strangers.

That day Mr. Ho, our host, tells us what features
Chinese men most admire in women: *oval face*
dimples small mouth straight nose

That day, my companion is cranky.
I forget something in my room & again
I don't hear (or remember) what he's saying.

I give up! There must be something
neurologically wrong with you—
that you don't hear me.

That day, Mr. Ho explains astrological signs.
He asks ours. We tell him & he laughs,
Not the best match. Sorry—

Rind of the Ancient Marinade

Trudi Beckman

with apologies to Coleridge

It is an ancient Marinade,
And it smiteth one of three.
'By its thick brown sheen and sparkling cast,
Now wherefore smiteth me?

The refrigerator's door is opened wide,
And I am here to clean;
The students are gone, the exams are done:
Must I gaze on the scene?'

It holds her with its sticky grip,
"There was a soda," quoth it.
"Hold off! Unhand me, brown-beard goop!"
Eftsoons its tendril split.

It holds her with its sparkling cast—
The secretary stood still,
And listens, horrified and aghast:
The Marinade has its will.

"The soda was fizzy, the owner busy,
The refrigerator quite packed
In the freezer, in the crisper,
With kibbles stacked."

The secretary can not tarry,
Yet she cannot choose but stay;
And thus spake on that ancient brine,
The bright-sheened Marinade.

"And now the over-pack came, and it
Was insidious and small:
A tiny V-8 juice rolled back
And dropped us down the wall.

"And now there came both fizz and hiss,
And it grew wondrous strong:
And pressure built, like a tea
Kettle left on flame too long.

"And then there happe'd a hellish thing,
And it would stay for ever:
For all was cursed, as seams were burst
That held the soda still a-quiver.

"Day after day, night after night,
I stuck, under racks and crispers;
As sticky as a candied child
Gobbling on a candied Snickers.

"Soda, soda, every where,
And all the fizz did shrink;
Soda, soda, every where,
Not any drop to drink.

"The very seep did rot: O Christ!
That ever this should be!
Yea, slimy things did grow with mold
Upon that slimy scene."

"I fear thee, ancient Marinade!
I fear thy syrupy sheen!
And thou art wide, and rank, and brown,
As is Pope's Belinda's spleen!

I fear thee and thy sparkling cast,
And thy sticky slime so brown."—
"Fear not, fear not, thou secretary!
For scrubbing shall wear me down.

"Farewell, farewell! But this I say
To thee, thou secretary!
She cleaneth well, who worketh well
For profs and docs and on salary."

The Marinade, whose cast was bright,
Whose beard with age was green,
Is gone; and now the secretary
Turned from the crisper fresh-clean.

She went like one that hath been stunned,
And is of sense forlorn:
A wiser and more cynical woman
She rose the morrow morn.

Non-Heroic Couplets for Kim

Kate Bernadette Benedict

Again our screens display their daily smut:
Kardashian has snapped her ample butt

and there it is displayed for all to see,
so glossy, cleft, protuberant and free.

What shall we make of this famed derriere,
offered like some ripe humongous pear?

Are we to pop our eyes and beat our meat
to shameless selfie and unblushing tweet?

Or are we meant to idolize these buns
just like a bunch of pervy, pious nuns?

O strumpet of the pixel and the page!
O harlot of the present cyber age!

You've taxed and drained the world's attention span.
Rein in that ass, stop twerking, can your can!

Non-Heroic Couplets for Kim

Of Suffering and Idiots

Alan Berecka

All for one and one for all
                    —Alexandre Dumas

As a kid I could never understand why
my father went ballistic when my Uncle Ben
said something stupid. Everyone knew Ben
was an idiot, a good man of sorts, but limited
at best. In his clumsy attempts to impress,
Ben flashed his profound ignorance. The fact
that he dropped out in the third grade never
kept him from claiming that he had aced
calculus. Once when Ben overheard my aunt
and mother commiserating about that time
of month, he bragged as a kid on the farm
he had ridden a menstruation cycle
without training wheels before he had turned
six. Everyone laughed, but my father fumed.
He screamed, *Ben, you talk like a guy*
with a paper asshole! My wounded uncle
wept, my mother screamed, *Albert!*
and the rest of us sat there laughing,
wondering, *What the hell is a paper asshole?*

Today in a meeting, a psych professor
who is long on ego and short on brains
was holding our pointless committee hostage
yet again with his mindless prattling,
but when he said . . . *and I for one,*
the inane phrase sparked a rage
so hot in my core that it fried the filter
that normally sits between my mouth
and brain, and I found myself barking,
And I for one! What are you, some kind
of schizophrenic musketeer? The virgin silence
slowly filled with the titters of a few committee
members, while others stared at our table top,
as if they hoped the etiquette for exiting
the awkward situation I had caused
could be found in its fake veneer.
The prattling pedant blushed and hushed,
then he gave me that hurt – You're a real
asshole kind of look. And I thought, *Touché,*
d'Artagnan, but at least I'm not a paper one.

St. Peter's Square 1979
Alan Berecka

College kids half drunk on cheap spumante,
we decided to stand at the barricades
for hours. As the crowd grew behind us
so did our plan. The new Polish Pope
was returning from Mexico and would pass
within earshot. We knew that he was known
to stop and bless or converse with pilgrims
who spoke his native tongue. Since my mother's
parents came from Poland, the group looked to me,
but my vocabulary was bluer than the Pontiff's
eyes. I feared my broken second-hand Polish
was more likely to land me in the bottom
of some secret and dank Vatican dungeon
than it was to gain us a Papal audience.

Plan B, we decided to consult our foreign language
pocket travel guide. Short of receiving the Paraclete's
gift of tongues, phonetics became our only chance.
We leafed through the little Polish it offered, looking
for some phrase that even Americans could pronounce.
Happy with our choice, we practiced in unison
as if we were again pre-communicants chanting
the Baltimore Catechism until we had it right.

That night as the young Pope rode past
a few feet away, we shouted in our best Berlitz,
Where are you going with our baggage?

The passing years bent the Pope
in half and hid him behind a cold
plastic mask, but I still relive that night.
Often in a dream, I see his confused look
snap around to our direction, and I swear
I can hear him answer, *Too far, my son, too far.*

The Long Song of Jane E. G. Blanchard

Jane Blanchard

Ma nondimen, rimossa ogne menzogna,
tutta tua visïon fa manifesta;
e lascia pur grattar dov'è la rogna.
                    (Dante, *Paradiso*, XVII, 127-129)

Let us go then, you and I,
Since the morning is already flying by
Like the hare that races tortoise in the fable;
Let us go, by some predetermined path,
Despite the aftermath
Of sleepless stint in dormitory suite
Post evening boozy-schmoozy meet-and-greet:
Path that leads you to the ludicrous consequence
Of ridiculous pretense
To keep you from an underwhelming comment . . . .
So, do not say, "Never mimic."
Let us go and face each critic.

In the room the poets sit and pose
Waiting for which way the wind blows.

And indeed there will be time
For the mellow grass that grows along the path,
Releasing ease as much as it is able;
There will be time, there will be time
To compose such leaves for all the readers at your table;
There will be time for laughter and for wrath,
And time for commendation to show up
And pour a phrase of praise into your cup;
Time for each of us right here,
And time yet for a dozen reinventions,
And for a dozen mentions and intentions,
Before the drinking of a wine or beer.

In the room the poets sit and pose
Waiting for which way the wind blows.

And indeed there will be time
To ponder, "Do I care?" and, "Do I care?"
Time to retreat and return to where
I can write whatever works without fanfare—
(They will say: "How her style is really old!")
My images, my metaphors, deliberately unrolled,
My diction plain, appropriate, arranged in syntax well-controlled—
(They will say: "Too bad her rhyme is not more bold!")

Do I care
What any critic thinks?
In an hour there is time
For inventions and intentions which may lead ourselves to drinks.

For I have known them all already, known them all:
Have known sestinas, sonnets, villanelles,
I have measured much such formulated cells;
And I have known the eyes, the arms,
Have known their steely or their hairy charms.
So how should I presume?
Should I now assume more leg- or elbow-room,
Forget a cigarette
(Since all butt-end ashes fall),
And reapply perfume?

And so let us resume.
Let us begin again,
And if not force the moment to its crisis,
Explore the power of an hour,
Dare disturb the universe,
Let the eternal Footman hear us curse.
He has heard it all before.
And more.

I may not be a prophet,
But I am not a crab.
And I may not be royalty,
But I am not a prince's poppet.
Indeed I have my share of vices:
I dress in drab

And practice some housewifery.
So I am me.

Or I, I should have said.
And though I have not risen from the dead
I can talk jack and jane about what I have read.

So would it have been worth it, after all,
Would it have been worthwhile,
After lectures, readings, workshops,
After grasses, drinks, groupthinks, bad-asses,
The daily, nightly flips and flops,
If one, without a smile,
Should say, "That is not it, at all."

It might be quite worthwhile
To see me play the Fool and say, "What gall!"

I may be a Georgia peach
Who spends half her time at some sweet beach
Where oyster shells grace fine hotels,
But I do swear I do not care what mermaids sing,
Or mermen either,
Each to each, or none to neither.
I shall not drown
Despite a critic's frown.

Regrets
Jane Blanchard

We are most grateful for the chance,
whatever be the circumstance,
to meet and shoot the bull.
There is no easy way to state
that we must aim for later date—
our calendar is full.

*

Especially since our turn is due,
it is extremely good of you
to treat with wine and cheese.
We really hate to turn you down,
but we are scheduled to leave town—
a raincheck, if you please.

*

So sorry, but we must decline
your offer for next week at nine
of dinner and a show.
By that time we are counting sheep—
far stronger is our need for sleep
than our desire to go.

*

You always host an open house
for every friend and every spouse,
if not for every brat.
But we stay home on Christmas Eve
and hope to look up Santa's sleeve
or underneath his hat.

*

For better, worse, we cannot come
for cocktails, canapés, with some
acquaintances of yours.
Do raise a glass or two of cheer
and welcome yet another year
with utter snobs and bores.

*

Your supper club—all in cahoots—
want us to serve as substitutes
for any missing folk?
No gourmet meal can make amends
for such rude treatment by old friends—
your kindness makes us choke.

*

When hell is cold, when donkeys fly,
will we pay what you specify
in not-so-subtle print.
How inappropriate, we think,
to charge your guests for food and drink.
Good luck with that event!

*

A party for your day of birth!
You've lasted longer on this earth
than anyone expected.
If only we could join you then,
but as your far-from-favored kin,
we would feel too dejected.

*

A wedding—fourth?—what bliss to share!
The service—Book of Common Prayer—
is such a lovely text.
A long vacation in the sun
ensures our absence from this one.
We'll try to make the next.

*

Hark! Finally, we get the gist
of why we're kept on your guest list.
It's not mere obligation.
Instead, you know that we will choose
a valid reason to refuse
each vapid invitation.

Blood Moon
CL Bledsoe

Think about it like this: 1000 years ago, people
were killing each other over the weather. A bit
of debris burns in the sky and anyone who offends

has got to die, badly. The stress of a mortgage,
the guilt of poor parenting decisions, the scarcity
of mushrooms since that prophet moved to

the neighborhood; Jesus couldn't hit a punch line
to save his life and yet what lovely hair. I did not
spend my life not ripping the bleeding fucking

hearts from my neighbors' weak chests while
their pathetic wives wail on the god damned ground
so that you can tell me about astronomy

and whatever the fuck an umbra is. The moon
is where all of our hopes go to drown in the blood
of our malformed endeavors. No astronaut ever walked

on its surface; if he had, why would he ever come back?

Leaving Wisconsin
CL Bledsoe

There is a hole in my soul that can only
be filled by processed sugars and corn
syrup. The sticky things comfort me.
Preservatives keep my feelings
from festering while they sit on some
cobwebbed shelf. I don't know when
the hotpockets will ever reach bottom
but I've got to keep pouring them down
until they do. Otherwise, how will I ever
climb out? You don't understand;
if I lost weight, people would just want
to fuck me. And then, where would I be?

Two Arts
Daniel Bosch

Are you at a loss? Why not go get a Master's?
Hundreds of programs are filled up with intense
People like you, each class as good as last year's.

You'd *have to* write, that way. You'd grow to trust your
Teachers and peers, to whom you would make sense.
If I were at a loss, I'd get a Master's.

Your father will write checks so fast his
Pen will spit. He needs to tell his friends
People like you grow up, this year's not last year.

Your mother? Watch. She'll steep the Pastor's
Tea with Sebaldian references:
"Was lost . . . is found," "My Master's house," etc.

Think: two whole years – maybe three – on casters.
Free time to read and write and to experience
New people, each class as good as last year's.

Even if some of them are real bastards,
Most people like you, you know, *like* you,
And people like you won't last here.
What have you got to lose? Go get a Master's.

Happily Ever After

J. H. Bowden

Prince Charming, the one who worked on Beauty
Sleeping, was some special kind of creep:
wake her he did from a hundred year sleep
but he never meant to—what that cutie
did (after everything else) was kiss her,
God knows why, and—BOIINNGGG!—up opened her eyes.
He voided, then and there, between her thighs,
with his hands still under her blouse. Mister,
she said, What sort is it hustles maidens
who are dead? Passive, he said when he could,
he liked them passive, no complications,
no chit-chat. By then the whole castle stood
at her door. So they wed, lived, as they say,
happily. Except on nights when she'd play
dead.

After Delivering My Son to the Ex

Matthew Brennan

Almost thirteen hours and pounds of sweat
Later, I'm back in town, already full
Of missing him the next two months. Along
The road, sunflowers leaned like fishing poles,
Tilting toward the west, as if dark, strong

Currents were pulling the light down, down and out
Of reach. I hunger for my son who's got
Away. I stop at work to check the mail,
Wanting human contact, but find that
Man my wife has left me for; he fails

To see me, for his head's submerged into
The dumpster, like a well from which one drinks.
Quickly I open the door, then pause to quip,
"Looking for your lunch?" Just now it sinks
In: what he eats won't ever have to touch my lips.

Revisiting Vietnam (While Dining across the Room from General William Westmoreland at a Retirement Community)

Matthew Brennan

Although my hair's above the ears
And though it's growing gray,
Unwittingly my knee-long shorts
And naked legs betray

A hairy rebel's attitude.
Or so the general thinks.
My plate of buffet food in hand,
I go to get our drinks,

But then the hostess intervenes,
A human barricade,
Demands I don a navy blazer,
And says that "I'm afraid

You can't get up again or you'll
Make the general mad."
More than thirty years before
Not yet an undergrad,

I watched my elder Boomers protest
The war Westmoreland waged,
Fitting flowers into rifles
And making guards enraged.

And now as if I'd dodged the draft
And fled to Montreal,
I've pricked the old man's thinnest skin
Not trying to at all.

But as we leave and pass his table,
Though I say not a word,
The body language of my legs
Flips the prig the bird.

Credit
Cory Brown

the gift from two holes

the ass who lent it to you

and the one you're in

Birds, Bees, and Referees
Nathan Brown

In the interest of pedagogy,
let us not be too hasty
to dismiss the metaphorical
merits of a sport like football.

For it was the good hearts
and vocabularies of ESPN
commentators who taught me
what little I know about sex.

How to *slip around the edge*
of the defensive line and then,
from there, to *push up inside*
without an *illegal use of hands*.

How the best we can hope for
is *narrowing the gap* so that
we get some *good penetration*
while maintaining *ball security*.

And what solid advice it is,
just before the snap, to always
*make sure and keep a close
eye on the tight end*.

That one has become
second nature to me now,
though I do worry about getting
called for *unsportsmanlike conduct*.

Yet, in my *aging defense*, it's not
my fault – all this *heavy traffic*
of *young recruits* running around
and *looking so fresh in training camp*.

I'll admit that when I was younger,
I could never figure out why
they were always carryin' on
about how *that hole was so big*.

They got so excited, they would
fumble all over their adjectives:
gaping hole . . . a *gigantic hole* . . .
or my favorite: *big-time hole*.

This was usually when they'd start
talking about that *huge turnover
late in the third quarter* and *what
a difference that made in the game.*

After *engaging the quarterback,*
he always got *nailed from behind,*
which often left the offense
backed up in the end zone.

From there, it became a litany
of how the defense had fully
dominated in the backfield,
which *forced it down the middle.*

At this point, all I cared about
was the *two-minute warning,*
just hoping *there'd be no official
review before the clock ran out.*

Still, It's important to say to all
the women I've loved: football
is the reason I know that *off-sides,*
chop-blocks, and *hands to the face,*

but especially *encroachment,*
holding, and that *jumping
into the Neutral Zone* are fouls
and therefore result in penalties.

And that *in order to win this game,*
we must *work together as a team.*

Humble Pie Café

Denise C. Buschmann

Open 24/7

Today's Breakfast Special
$ Owning up

scrambled
eggs

jam on
toast

buttered
grits

dose of
crow*

No Meat Substitutions

Make Your Mark in the World
Don Kingfisher Campbell

All you need is a marker
Or even better a pocket knife
Then choose a public place
Maybe a mall or library
A school would be best
Now, wait for a lonely minute
And write your name large
(Use a code if you fear arrest)
Give yourself points for style
If you feel you have artistic ability
Clamber over a wall at night
So you can colorfully spray, impress
Passersby to see what you've left behind
They will comment on it like art
Some may grumble, call for a janitor
But don't let those painted squares
Stop you from achieving notoriety
Continue to alter original designs
Until you grow tired of the game
And settle into more mature activities
Like using a gun or a bomb
If you become smart someday
You might have a chance to accomplish
The status of white collar criminal
All you need is a brain

Buying Sneakers
Michael Cantor

The designer's iconic plaid on this canvas high top lace-up sneaker ($275) is hand sprayed to give it a slight degradé effect.
—Advertisement in the *New York Times*

The look I want is slightly *dégradé*;
aloof and elegant, yet with a flair
that hints of darkness in an offhand way;

exquisite, yes, but not too *recherché*,
and at the same time, more than *ordinaire*.
That look! I want it *slightly dégradé*,

just right to make the scene in St. Tropez,
or stir up gossip of an old *affaire*
with hints of darkness and the offhand way

that one once murmured, *je suis désolée*,
and left a lover twisting in the air.
The look is wan, and *jeune*, and *dégradé*.

Now that my *Nikes* have become *passé*
I need a *soupçon* of aggrieved despair
that hints of darkness in an offhand way,

so show me something that is *distingué*,
that cries *regardez-moi,* and makes you dare
to look. And want me slightly *dégradé!*
I hint at darkness in an offhand way.

The Elements of Style
Michael Cantor

In formal writing, the future tense requires shall for the first person, will for the second and third. The formula to express the speaker's belief regarding his future action or state is I shall; I will expresses his determination or his consent. A swimmer in distress cries, "I shall drown; no one will save me!" A suicide puts it the other way: "I will drown; no one shall save me!" In relaxed speech, however, the words shall and will are seldom used precisely; our ear guides us or fails to guide us, as the case may be, and we are quite likely to drown when we want to survive and survive when we want to drown.

—Strunk and White, *The Elements of Style*

I know that I shall scream to all who pass,
"I'm fucking drowning—save my ass!"
And hope they never heard of William Strunk,
for if they have, I'm fucking sunk.

Dangerous Women
Alan Catlin

"I did it the modern way.
A Jane Fonda Special:2
a tuck here and a tuck there,
a little breast augmentation,
some Botox injections and
you're as good as new. Better.
Workout tapes are for losers."
She said, a mature woman of
indeterminate age somewhere
between late 40's and ready-at-
a-moment's notice for cryonic
preservation, smoking E-cigarettes
at a hotel lounge bar and drinking
a good, full bodied Pinot Noir.
Her female companion was
similarly attired in revealing
top and short skirt, her hair one
bottle short of albino white,
claiming she liked a natural
look, as in making the best of
what you were born with, which
must have been Jayne Mansfield's
body with a new head sewn on.
It was easy to imagine an investment
firm of exes working mega billable
hours to keep both of them in designer
duds and the best jewelry money
could buy, both of them three-quarters
of the way into a mean drunk,
wanting love in the worst way
but incapable of finding it, as they
surveyed the room for likely
bedmates. Empty sex was better
than no sex at all they told themselves,
freshening their faces in the Ladies,
splitting a snort of crank to take
the edge off, primed and ready
for what the night would provide.

Another Art
Catherine Chandler

after Elizabeth Bishop's "One Art"

The art of keeping isn't hard to master;
so many things seem filled with the intent
to be kept that their keeping's no disaster.

Keep something every day. Accept the fluster
of keeping up with the Joneses, opulent
though they may be. Charge it to Master

Card. And keep your cool. Don't bluff and bluster.
Keep track of time, your moment's monument
to order wrought from chaos and disaster.

He kept a mistress, overtaxed his rooster,
and so I told him, *Keep in touch,* then sent
Prince Charming packing. Piece of cake to master.

I kept two children (lovely ones!), the toaster,
the house, the SUV; and when he went
I kept the faith. No sad, ill-starred disaster.

So, round up every heartache you can muster—
a squad, a company, a regiment—
a castle keep of slings and arrows. Master
these. Or else you're headed for disaster.

The Prison Farm Doctor, Louisiana 1923

Robert Cooperman

"Doctor say better stop ballin' that jack,
If I live five years I gonna bust my back . . ."
—"Easy Wind" (Robert Hunter)

I was caught giving abortions,
and the one who died just had to be
a state senator's darling daughter.
Lucky I'm not breaking my back
on a work crew, but have a cottage
on the grounds, and a housekeeper
to warm my bed, cook and keep
my shack the safe side of filthy.

The warden can depend on me
when men get shot trying to escape,
and if I botch an appendix operation
or two, who's going to miss a convict,
especially the ones without families?

But now they bring this prisoner in,
his jack-hammer jumping from his grip;
I had the devil's time wiring his jaw;
somehow he managed to suck down
cheap wine while I was working.

"Look, my man," I pointed at his chest,
"stop drinking or you'll be dead in five years."

He just laughed, and drooled a last swig.
We shared another few bottles; by the time
I meandered home, my housekeeper
was on me, mean-tempered as a gator.

"For showin' your ugly, drunken mug
when I've fixed you a decent dinner.
You can forget about the nasty tonight,"
she snapped. But of course relented.

What else is there to do here?

The Un-Promise of Pheromones
Sarah Cortez

Athena Institute must have
phenomenal pheromone products
since a small glass vial
rates a ninety-nine dollar
and fifty cent check
(or money order) despite
being unscented, unguaranteed,
and not an aphrodisiac. Right

here, human pheromone results
are documented in a national
weekly magazine with a
bold, glossy cover usually
un-associated with (human)
biology and/or erectile function.

In fact, actual testimonials
attached to actual re-orders
from Boyd (Montana)
or Kyle (Massachusetts) state
this after-shave additive works
on eight out of ten women. Incredible
(unguaranteed) sex-appeal
even to a wife or a complete
(female) stranger! Yes,

her pupils will dilate,
conversation will sparkle,
hearts will tilt toward
each other, and Athena
(Institute) rests assured
you'll feel the higher octane
in all the secret, swell places.

The Red Dress

Sherry Craven

A silk thread from my red dress,
caught on your heart when you left.
I saw the crimson unraveling,
like last year's dreams,
sailing away into the night
until I could see scarlet no more,
leaving me standing
naked and embarrassed,

but if you should go again,
I will snare you on my
pearls, which are knotted
like my heart, between
each delicious concentric sphere,

so when the strand is broken,
only one gem is lost.
I keep the rest.

Envying the Solipsist
Dallas Crow

after Troy Jollimore's "The Solipsist"

Isn't your solipsist a straw man
(and not in the *Wizard of Oz* sense)?
I'm no philosopher, no bird watcher,
neither carpetbagger nor muckraker,
no bandersnatch, no chatterbox (really!),
but I can recognize blood, tell the hunter
from the hunted. I can grasp at straws
as well as any drowning man. I was married
to pain, then untimely ripped in most unseemly
fashion from that blinding bondage, and
here's the thing I've learned about divorce:
if there are kids, it doesn't undo the
til death do us part part. So here I am:
a smart ass, but no smarty pants, no wiser
for my wounds (or words), wondering
why I have to wake every morning
hating my ex-wife. No, I know why
I hate her. The reasons are legion.
What I want is a pox upon the ex,
an exorcism of my invaded unconscious,
an exoneration, an escape.
Oh, I envy the solipsist, impossibly
fictional configuration that he is.

Christmas Letter
Chip Dameron

Last summer
my daughter
blah blah blah

This boasting—
tone deaf and
torturous,
unrelieved
by humor—
overtunes
his kids' real
talents, and
no friend cares
to be awed
by the man's
narcissis-
tic braying.
We'd almost
rather hear
someone died—
got real drunk
and fell off
a ladder—
and no last
immortal
whispers, please.

The Hat
William Virgil Davis

Instead of handing you your hat
or putting it on your head for you,
I put it on my own head.

I felt as if it had always been mine,
and I walked out into the sunlight,
the brim turned down to shade my sight.

All day I had such strange thoughts,
and that night, I am certain, I made
love to another man's wife. Yours.

Poem Not Published in the *Ark River Review*, 1974, Vol. 2, #4
Paul Dickey

I have been writing this poem all of my life, and something
last night reminded me of it. Buddy and I had been drinking
Scotch. Liz was telling me about her daughter's endeavors.
My next wife wasn't there. She implied she would never
be again. The Wichita literati were playing monopoly
on the other side of the Ark River. We called Iowa City
to talk to Phil Haskell to see why last week *The New York
Review of Books* said we can't write fiction anymore.
Buddy was thinking that if we stopped writing poetry
& wrote fiction again, it might be more real. Phil was at a party.
He might call back. We called James Mecham to cover
our story. Just in case. He guessed it'd be okay if we came over
for a quick drink. A week before I'd written a joke to submit
to the *Ark River Review*. I thought the Eds would see the wit
(and impress Diana, I admit). It was called *Poem Submitted
to the Ark River Review, 1974.* It was adolescent. Mecham asked
if we wanted some wine. Buddy did. Mecham placed a glass
between Diana and me. She was with Jonathan Katz.
Diana (no, this time I mean the goddess) was putting together
a jigsaw puzzle. She apologized if it was too easy a metaphor.
There might have been some sarcasm. I had written a poem
last week, *And So It Happened Near the Time of Jeroboam,*
after we work-shopped her *Jephthah's Daughter,* so it seemed
important if it was Diana's wine or mine. I never dreamed
she'd drink my wine. Diana didn't care anymore. Buddy and I
were drinking Scotch, and I knew if I mixed it with wine,
I'd have to pretend to be sick. Buddy told Jonathan Katz
that he could tell Katz wasn't at all from Wichita. The brass
at the *Ark River Review* was from Brooklyn! I had told Buddy
in the car that my wife knew Katz well in Ohio, and now we
are in a second stanza. But don't give up yet on the *Ark's* lit.
Sure, there's little subtext, no metaphor. Get used to it.
It's just life. This ain't Professor Katz' Moby Dick seminar.
Yeah, take that, Jonathan. This ain't your Moby Dick seminar.
You think this isn't even poetry? What can I tell you?
(In twenty years, someone came out of the blue
and called it *creative nonfiction.*) I watched the goddess stack LPs
on the record player. Buddy wanted to leave and it was
his car. Now it is Sunday morning. My ex-wife meant to play
golf. At Buddy's, she confessed she had to go, let's just say,
camping on the river with her ex-husband. I want my coffee black.
This is an apology to *Di and Jonathan* for how I act. I want to go back
to the tent and sleep it off. But I am still waiting for the call,
to hear Phil say it is okay to write fiction again and add "Oh, Paul,
by the way, get real. The *Ark* won't publish either me or you.
We're a postmodern *reductio ad absurdum* on their latest issue."

Reply to the Poetry Editor Who Asked What Her Readers (Likely Only Writers) Wanted from *Great Poem Review*'s Newsletter

Paul Dickey

Thank you for asking, Emily, but there
is no answer to such a question.
It is too much like asking why some poems
are published and others are rejected.
I'm sure you meant well,

You thought a question deserved an answer,
one that might further the discussion.
No doubt, it was a question someone
in an editors' meeting already
has answered many times, and thus

forever will be their editorial secret.
It left you feeling not so much rejected
as unsatisfied. I too know that feeling.
There are no answers to many questions
in this artsy world we have chosen

to live in together. There may even be
no reasons for things—like why would I
send a poem like this to you in an email,
where you cannot even consider it
for publication when I could have

submitted it online for only a $3 fee?
Unpublished poets too ask unanswerable
questions. You almost said it yourself.
What does *Great Poem Review* want from *Paul Dickey*?
One simple poem that saves the dying language?

Or do you just want me to change my name?
You said yourself: "Seriously, I want to know."
But I can't ask. I should be satisfied

only to ask what did you hope for
when you sent out the call for submissions?

Michelangelo's secret prose poems?
I'm embarrassed to say it, but I'd like to know
what poems do for you, naked,
fully networking, in the darkness of night,
in the eternal distance between poem and editor.

But Emily, we've never met at a conference,
so this is all Rilkean I know, and all I can say is:
We regret that your last newsletter does not
fit our current needs, but we appreciated
the opportunity to consider your work.

Socio's Path
Colin Dodds

Even if there is no community,
there is an intersecting nihilism
among the old and young men, like myself,
of the business community

Gone to jobs that take a half-hour to explain,
men who like to be called president, who harness each other,
and lie about who harnessed who until their lies become true,
struggle earnestly to reconcile buy-low, sell-high with the golden rule

Even if there is no love,
but there is the interlocking damage
of a love affair

From the Catholic Church to the AMA,
there's no such thing as an honest organization
And the suspicion burgeons among us dear, dear friends,
that there is no such thing as honesty

In the nave of the restaurant, you and I
boast of, and apologize for, how well we eat,
under the curse of the cow and the man who brings the cow,
who have each been reduced to warning us:
Every species is warped by its prey

Armor Vincit Omnia

Tom Dodge

The shut-in, Honey Suggs, will seldom go outside his house these days and then to only feed the dogs and smoke.
The mailman asked him, said, "What happens if you go about a mile down
      to the store and buy your smokes or get a Coke?"
"My breath hangs in my gullet and my body cells implode much as they do when you bring letters from the IRS
      about my gas lease tax.
So with all due respect to commerce and humanity I stay at home in deference to my health and try to mind my
      own beeswax."

Because of fear he missed all funerals and weddings, birthdays and reunions, also every other family get-together
      or occasion
but never missed a month of sending his long-suffering wife to Oklahoma
      to buy cigarettes at Chickasaw Indian Nation.
They're tax-free and they're cheap but never mind the hardship
      on his wife and cost of gasoline.
She doesn't go these days because she got lung cancer and she died from taking in his secondary smoke and
      nicotine.

Two characters in books he likes that act like him were made by Shakespeare and some say Capote:
Boo Radley was a recluse, Hamlet was as well but complicated, filled with doom, too wan and gay and quotey.
Proust was still another and admired as were that housebound Emily and   Howard Hughes, and Hawthorne,
      who remained inside for also quite a while.
They're all loved now due to their fame but Honey isn't, due to there being no such word, he says: "agoraphile."

To save his life such as it is his widowed sister put a paper bag around his head to shield him from the fearsome
      sight of bridges, cars, and
      overpasses,
And took him to a doctor far out in the sticks so he would be protected from the sight of human beings which he
      calls jackasses.
She'd brought him to her farm to live with her and her nine dogs and her
      gas lease.

After she died from cancer too her sons then sold the farm by lots except
      the one where Honey lives now with his handicapped disabled niece.

So Honey goes outside to smoke in order not to kill his niece and sits and ponders aspects of his aspects of his
      guilt for two already dead but smokes nevertheless.
He loves his niece and helps her cook and clean and even lifts her in and out the tub and from her chair into her
      car so she can go get groceries and cigaress.
In fact they're copasetic and compatible as they could ever be as man and wife.
She even likes to read his Clancy novels and watch "Night Court" with him on TV and feels she's needed for the
      first time in her life.

My Quirky Voice

George Drew

I sent my poems to you and after six months
you sent them back. I know what you want
because you said so: deep psychology,
true emotion. You did enjoy my quirky voice,
you said, and thanked me. I thank you back,
for your promptness. Honestly, though,
I know what you want to know: my little sins
and self-deceptions, crises of identity;
my peculiar peccadilloes: betrayals, thefts,
chicaneries, crimes of gender and ego,
Freudian imbroglios, petty misdemeanors
of mind and heart, ethical sellouts, lapses
into first this deadly sin, then that. You want,
in short, me undressed; me stripped, unzipped
and shaken out, exposed the way a nutcase did
himself to one of my girlfriends on a street
in England. God knows, I've tried tearing away
all my defenses the way the wind does leaves
from their branches in October. Just today I
went to the mall and stood before a mannequin.
The mannequin was naked and without form,
and I stood for a long while, trying to likewise
pare myself down to bare essentials, to reveal
more than what is skin-deep. I have to tell you,
though, like the trees in autumn, after the leaves
have been stripped away, what remains is gray
and bare, a skeleton of limbs and twigs. Thanks,
again, for your best wishes and for taking time
to hand-write a note in ink. With apologies
for being so boringly normal, I am,
                                        Truly yours.

Nearly

George Drew

Nearly is always close to enough, but not quite.
Otherwise, *nearly* would be *is*. It isn't,
but it isn't not, either. Take the time
Carl Cragston pissed in my thermos
and tied it to the top of a tall birch.

Retrieving it, which symmetrically speaking,
meant going up to bring it down,
was harder going up than coming down.
Nearly symmetrical, but not quite, again;

also what happened next. Hard work,
like climbing, requires hydration,
which I accomplished with a big swallow,
not knowing it was spiked with piss. Carl knew,
and as milk dribbled down my chin told me,
then grinned as wide as his own ass would
one day be, and helping its evolution along,
I knocked him onto it. He grinned again,
and guffawed; I neither grinned nor guffawed.
Another nearly symmetrical, but not quite.

When Carl stood up I would have on the spot
cold cocked his miserable self,
but that would have been perfection,
and I'm not a perfect man. Imperfectly

I cursed, and he cursed back. He ran his mouth,
I walked away. Symmetrical, and not.

Invocation for an Acceptance to Graduate School
Millard Dunn

All praise and thanksgiving to almighty God,
Creator of the heavens and the earth
And of all who live thereon,
And special praise and thanksgiving
For the creation of human beings,
And academic communities, faculty,
Staff, and administrators, and for those
Who teach, and those who learn, and those
Who would take us by the hand to help us
Do both better. We ask your forgiveness
For those hurtful things we have done to one another,
Or not done to one another when we should have,
And especially your forgiveness for the formation
Of academic and administrative committees
Which have wasted everyone's time
And brought great bitterness among us
And subjected us to University Politics
And meetings beyond number. But chiefly
We come before you today to ask
Your blessing on this child, this young woman,
Who, because of her father's wisdom and experience
Should know better but has decided anyway—
Led no doubt by your greater wisdom
And purpose—to earn an advanced degree
And to toil among the academics. Guard her
From jealousy, envy, backbiting, gossip,
Complaints to the dean, and all other snares
And traps that academics set for each other.
Guide her into the paths of graciousness
And generosity that cross every campus,
No matter how cleverly we have hidden them.
Bless her in her work and in her play,
And grant that all of us gathered here
Receive such grants, sabbaticals, raises,
And promotions as we are needful of
To do your work and to build an impressive
Retirement portfolio. All of this we ask
In the name of him whose teaching evaluations
Were excellent, but who did not publish,
And who went to Glory at your right hand
Untenured, except in your grace
And love everlasting. Amen.

Loaves and Fishes in an Election Year
Millard Dunn

Men's Prayer Breakfast at JC's,
A new restaurant, family oriented:
An even dozen gathered here
Agreeing, once again, that they

Alone are saved and, being saved,
That they alone are safe. They spend
Their hour talking politics:
Scrambled Eggs asks, "Do you think

He'll win?" Pancakes with Extra Syrup
Says, "Hell, he can't lose."
Several scowl at his language but soon
Get back to eating. "His opponent's

Pretty smart," Two Eggs
Over Easy offers. "She don't
Stand a chance," Sausage and Gravy
Says, his mouth still full,

"Christ, she supports that
Minimum Wage mumbo jumbo."
Oatmeal looks up from his bowl.
"I'd have to lay off half my staff,"

He says, "just to stay where I am."
"And where, exactly, is that?" their pastor
Asks. He's having only coffee.
(He ate breakfast at 4 AM

In the hospital cafeteria.) "He's
Doing OK," Pancakes with Extra
Syrup says, "New wife,
New house, new car, new . . . ."

"That's enough," Oatmeal says.
Then Scrambled eggs says, "But it *is*
True." "The Lord indeed has blessed
My business with success," Oatmeal

Whispers, stopping his spoon half-
Way to his mouth to get it out.
"Say that again!" thunders
From the other end of the long table.

"The Lord indeed . . ." Oatmeal begins,
But everybody gets it. Someone
Else from the other end of the table,
His plate already cleaned, chimes in

"Darn right!" And from another,
"He worked hard for every penny of it."
"No," a new voice says
From a nearby table, "*they* work

Hard and *he* gets almost
All the pennies." A stunned silence
While the Prayer Breakfast turns together
To face this voice, to find its face.

"Sorry, Preacher," the man says,
"But it *is* true, if you believe
There's such a thing as truth." "Do
We know you?" Oatmeal

Asks. "I do," the pastor says,
"From way back. How are you, John?"
"Doin' OK. Call me Jack,
Like you used to, back when

We were kids." "You know this man?"
Oatmeal asks, incredulous. "We grew up
Together," the pastor says, "but
We've taken different paths. Haven't we,

Jack?" "Towards the same end, I hope,
Or at least close," Jack says.
"We should talk about that sometime," the pastor
Says, "maybe over lunch."

"I'd love to. Give me a call, unless
You want to set a time right
Now." The pastor glances down
The length of his table. These people

Pay his salary. "I'll call
You," he says. "You've got
My number?" "Yes." And now he knows
This Prayer Breakfast—to a man—has his.

Talking in My Sleep
Maureen DuRant

Mornings, over the coffee and paper, you report
my nightly conversations, my unconscious words
muttered in bed. You, posing as friend-of-the-court,
give testimony: "Last evening, my wife said, *Birds
in the house mean death is on the way.*" Sighing, I start
to explain, and the toast snaps up. "Just two nights
ago, my wife whispered, *Hands to yourself or sit apart.*"
Eggs sputter in the skillet, yolks swirled into the whites.
Now a game you love, monitoring nocturnal sounds,
my declarations. "*I like you both; it's a toss-up!*"
You, tuned in like a tired FBI agent waiting for grounds
to prosecute, eavesdropping on private, juicy gossip,
listen closely to my advice, go to sleep. Long ago
I stumbled. Don't learn what you do not want to know.

Genitals

Andrea Eames

There is no language for them
that is not clinical, antiseptic,
or coy and embarrassed,
or obscene.

They are surreptitious
a stray dog or pussycat
that follows you home
and hangs around
waiting to be fed;
the members who left before the band got famous.

They are hidden, like dinner's green vegetables
tucked in a napkin.

They are antennae, quivering and tiptoed –
the radar of a bat,
the blind sense of a mole
the whiskers of a cat.

They burrow and nose between our legs,
give a running commentary on our day's affairs.

They are
the hecklers in the back row.

They are dirty jokes,
God's punchline to the Adam and Eve gag.

Urban Myth

Andrea Eames

It always happened
to a friend of a friend—
I heard it whispered.

Like sightings of Elvis,
though, to be honest,
he put on more of a show

If you had taken your act
to Vegas, now, you
wouldn't be in this mess. You

make it all sound like
Christmas, presents under
the tree on your birthday,

presents for everyone.
More like pass the parcel;
we move you round

the circle, taking off
your wrappings one by
one but we're left

with a pile of empty
papers and no damn
prize. Son of god my ass.

Mickey's Mao Suit
Meg Eden

on Beijing Shijingshan amusement park

Mickey insists, I'm not a mouse! I'm just
a cat with unusually round ears.

Mickey, cut the bull crap. We all know
copyright infringement when we see it.
Even the costume teens admit their stolen
identities. It's only the overworked mothers
who snap like socialists:

Shouldn't others be able to use
those characters besides Disney?

Seven refugee dwarfs with careless
eyes wave to the cameras, which translates:
Always protect your social security numbers.
You never know who they'll make love to.
The dwarfs cluster by weeping woman statue,
bearing trademark Snow White tendencies.

Mickey tells me, Disneyland is too
far away, please come here—
But tourist evidence reveals
a loss more fragile—

If we are name-stealers,
then call me Wendy Zhang.
Let me be twenty poets.
Let me run whole-heartedly
through pavement-seas
with this dangerous freedom.

Everything Flows
Chris Ellery

After closing the tavern
we drove to the big bridge
and sat on the tailgate
listening to the water
against the pilings.

The air was so still he said
the wind must be sleeping.
I said I should be sleeping.
He said he should be sleeping.
We went on listening.

He said just listen
to the sound of the water.
I said yeah
that's really something.
He waited a minute.

Then yawning he added
you know that sound
is as much the sound
of the bridge
as it is the water.

Ode to Suzzanne

Joe Garland

It is said of an old man's nose
That it always continuously grows
My wife's butt
Is in the same rut
I'll never admit that it shows

Clothes Make the Musician

Claudia Gary

Protégée, dear,
skip the brassiere
and bare your shoulders, toes.
Now hold that deafening pose

and have no fear:
critics won't hear
the burblings and mutterings
your bow makes on the naked strings.

How Long, O Lord, How Long?
Mark Goad

My morose old friend was complaining of the pain
and uselessness of being 89 years old.

I, stupidly, mentioned
"Methuselah lived to be 969 years old."

"My God," he said, "how sad. What did he do
with the last nine hundred years?"

The Lies of Poets

Mark Goad

Poets are poor liars
unless they are talking about themselves
or their poems.

Other than these, they've got
not a lying bone in their bodies.

Sometimes they do lie to lovers
and former lovers. When absolutely necessary,
to their children. Sometimes
to themselves. And if, unfashionably,
they believe in God, sometimes
to God, too.

Other than these, they've got
not a lying bone in their bodies and

probably, I certainly wouldn't
lie to you.

The Other Writers Block
Lyman Grant

1
A student stands in my doorway
confessing some desperate
"blockage in my creative faculties"
and before I can inquire
if she really talks like that
or if she picked it up, like Strep,
by listening too closely to exalted professors
at our "institution of higher learning,"
she tilts her head and does something
funny with her eyes and then
her lips, and says I wouldn't
understand, that nothing like that
could ever happen to me.

2
Remembering unfinished poems
from the beginning of the term,
I try to name once again
the stack of papers on the front
right corner of the desk,
I call it "a mountain," then
"dunghill." The phrase "a ringing"
telephone I don't want to answer,"
runs through my head. Next
it's "a bouquet." The pen scratches
on a piece of scrap "the tears
of black desire in a white sea,"
and crosses it out. Finally, I hear
"sprouting voices singing the irradiated
waltz in the polluted compost
of the twentieth century." The hour
passed, I put away my pen and
amble to my morning composition
class, leaving the "metaphors"
ungraded and unremarked.

3
Even though it's my office hour,
I imagine that, if I shut
the door and stanch the flow
of words not my own, some trickle
from the reservoir of either hope or
memory might moisten the dry
arroyos of "my personal voice."

The lessons, "write every day,"
"write the things you care about,"
"write from your own perspective"
begin to crowd the corridor and soon
one of them gets rowdy and rips
from the closed door my favorite
wry *New Yorker* cartoon.
Then all hell breaks loose and pretty
soon James Wright comes barreling
in screaming, "I have wasted my life,"
and Rilke returns from the realm
of angels, whispering, "You must
your life change." I begin
to envision myself an astronaut
or a penitent, anything cut off
and alone, a piece of string,
an insect husk. And just when I'm
about to yell they must silence
themselves and stand in line
like everything else, someone knocks,
and before I can ignore "him or her,"
a student opens the door and asks,
"Have you graded my essay, yet?"

Summer Returns to Texas

Lyman Grant

Summer is not your Yankee friend who comes to visit
once a year for a long weekend of greasy enchiladas
and too many margaritas and dancing late at Stubb's,
the one who troubles your husband, that puts him
in that state about all the time he's had to spend with kids.
But he gets over it. He always does because the sex is hotter
for a week or two, at least. You're sad to see her go,
late Tuesday morning, still hung over but laughing,
driving cautiously away in her Honda, windows down,
her freshly showered blonde hair shining, except at the roots.
No, Summer is your cousin, the daughter of the drunk
uncle, who never really had a chance to grow up right.
She shows up in early spring. Her parents have thrown
her out, again, with no place else to go. You're her last
hope, her only choice. And you're so kind. She stands
in your perfect kitchen, the fridge door open, forking
leftovers from the Tupperware, wiping her hands
on her dirty t-shirt. Drinking beer. She says she'll get a job.
She says she'll help out. She says you won't regret it.
She won't stay long, not like last year when she upset
everyone at Thanksgiving. That was bad, she knows.

These Are Things I've Been Wanting To Tell You
Lyman Grant

I don't give a shit about chipotle sauce.
I don't care where these peppers are grown
or special techniques best chefs use
to reduce heat and remove seeds,
to enhance that smoky flavor
so reminiscent of Indian fires,
which neither you nor I have ever smelled.

What I care about,
the only thing I've ever god damned cared about,
is the one tiny droplet of sienna cream
on the edge of your red lips, smiling.

And I only pretend to believe that Miller Lite is piss
and the only beer I'll ever drink again,
ever, ever in my entire life is some micro-brewed amber ale
made with Austrian hops and spring Canadian snowmelt,
produced only in limited quantities, but by some miracle
is available in Albertsons throughout the South.

But I told you the truth
when I said the butterfly
that paused, migrating North,
on the empty ice chest
three days after our spring party
made me see the unfolding joy of our life together.

And I couldn't give a flying fuck
about fabrics and furniture,
about what Martha Stewart or *Architectural Design*
would do with our space,
about how angels, or was it gargoyles, are in or out,
about how you want a room that Henryk Gorecki,
not Philip Glass, could settle into,
about how you just can't go to the Pottery Barn
now that they've opened a store in our podunk town.

I just want to hear once more the Shaker tune
you hummed to yourself in sunlight,
holding from your garden a single rose,
wearing those stupid green plastic clogs
that you mail ordered from Smith and Hawken.

Edward's Indecisiveness

Jonathan Greenhause

Edward was born into:
  a) a strict Orthodox family,
  b) a sect worshipping small winged animals,
  c) a family of punch-loving born-again somethings,

but from the time he was:
  a) little more than a fetus,
  b) immersed in his quarter-life crisis,
  c) recovering from a gender-change operation,

he was aware he'd become:
  a) a reoccurring Tibetan Buddhist,
  b) a game-show host tired of playing games,
  c) a snake-charmer afraid of snakes,

& so he searched for meaning by:
  a) dismantling Grandfather clocks & prewar aircraft.
  b) abstaining from half of his sexual activities.
  c) studying the lost art of commercial Mad-Libbing.

As a result, Edward knew:
  a) how long it takes for objects to fall 100 meters,
  b) the importance of seeming smart,
  c) that he was trapped inside this particular poem,

& with this knowledge, he could:
  a) unify general relativity & quantum mechanics,
  b) sing bass at the Metropolitan Opera House,
  c) make pancakes on a street corner in Bangkok,

but time passed, & Edward could never:
  a) incorporate metaphors into his rhyme schemes,
  b) turn down mediocre literary prizes,
  c) tie everything together at the end of this poem,

or maybe he could.

Vote for Me

Jonathan Greenhause

Vote for me   because I might be who you think I am,
& I don't kill puppies   nor mug old ladies
nor make a mockery   of our beloved constitution.
I'm not saying my opponent does,   but I'm not saying she doesn't.
I'm not saying she doesn't dream of installing a brutal shadow regime
to kidnap your parents   & turn them into fascist zombies.
I'm not saying any of this,   but I'm not refuting it.
I don't run drugs across the border   (or at least
haven't been convicted of it)   & don't poison the waterways
nor cross-dress   nor condone marriage with farm animals,
though if I did,   there'd be a good reason for it,
that term *animal husbandry*   always confusing me.
I believe in rights & freedom   & cheese-fries & flying kites,
& I love to kiss babies,   their skin so soft
sometimes I dream of it   & wake up in a cold sweat.
This is a new dawn in our country;   & it's a new sunrise, too,
& all the new things   accompanying a new sunrise.
It's like getting rid of all the things you didn't like
& creating a private country   all for yourself.
If you vote for me,   you'll have unlimited chocolate
as well as sex   & cotton-candy   & circus elephants,
& you'll be young again,   & your grandparents   (if they're dead,
God bless their souls),   will rise from their graves
& grow young again, too,   & they'll vote for me
& not for that woman   who says she's not a communist,
but really,   who knows?

Eureka! Corner Drugstore, Slushy March Afternoon
Maryanne Hannan

The clerk rings up my two prescriptions, super-strength cough syrup, Aloe-treated tissues, and a $6.99 "Sincere Sympathy on the Loss of Your Mother" card for a friend—then advises me to enjoy the day. Shocked by the coexistence of her rational exterior and illogical yak, I abandon the obvious response—In what universe could that happen, you pasty-faced trilobite? I reassess, discover she is me, my Ideal Self, fully realized, the Real Deal. She doesn't just talk augmented reality; she lives it! Time to cheer up, quicken my inner Queen of Lemonade, leave old Norman Vincent Peale panting in my sniffly, sneezy dust and renew that Robotics for Everyone subscription. Who knows? Maybe someday I could love a low-footprint cyberdog.

Legal Disclaimer
Michelle Hartman

All characters and events in this publication, other than those clearly in the public domain are fictitious and any resemblance to actual persons, living or dead is purely coincidental.

Except for you, Eddie I meant every word
I wrote about you. And as for my inbreed
happy-clappie in-laws, most of whom are outlaws
I don't have to worry because
the majority of you cannot read.
I did not leave out those marvelous blind dates
    sweaty, butt-crack guy
      and peely, unibrow dude
who promised to bomb my womb with his big cannon.
So while I'm clearing the poetic air
Fred, there is no such thing as necrolepsy and
Salmonella Faye, stop telling people that your name
is French, your family is white trash.
I've lived among the
    gilded vice of forgive-all, prosperity gospel
      haggard harpies, (yes, we stacked her but I'm making no promises)
and suicides adjacent, (really, the rate on my paternal side is ridiculous).
But all the rest of this conforms absolutely
with what the money-grubbing blood-sucking,
attorneys told me to write.

Eve in the New Millennium

Johnny Hartner

God, garden, only-game-in-town husband,
fruit-offering snake, the first day
      of existence
is too much to take in.
If the Mother of Sin had a day in court now
      her point would be well taken.
Well, nobody bothered to email, text or tweet me.
How was I to know? I had no voice mail saying
"Eve, WTF! He's the devil."
Thus, we can understand why no woman
      admits when she's wrong.
The permanent accoutrement of Eve's genes
they are all doomed to denial.
      Micromanaging any office, position of authority,
it's her way or the highway. If it all falls apart
and accused of being wrong now,
Bogart's "Well, I was misinformed"
for an answer is far more weighty
      but really no different
than yesteryear's "He made me do it"
for simple apple biting.

Stagecoach

Johnny Hartner

Like a John Wayne gunslinger
who's hung up his pistols for the last time,
retired at twenty-four, our neighborhood stripper,
        oh, excuse me, exotic specialist,
has nestled for 44s, her "girls," the twins,
inside their holster.
        So now the only flesh parade
comes around the block at five o'clock:
the evening stroll of baby carriage, armlength brats;
and we, the good ole boyz in da hood,
unhappy horndogs, do miss those paps!
        But this Ice Princess pays us no never mind,
her nose now up in the air, a cold Gypsy Rose Lee.
From hoi polloi to hoity toit, the *nouveau bitch*
is too good now to share her goods.
        And we're just sad, the horndogs of the hood.
Burly old prospectors,
        Festuslike from *Gunsmoke*,
we squint and spit tobaccky
as she be comin' round the mountain.
        "Boys, it's the stagecooch! She be right on time!"
Maybe if we're good little horndoggies
and not flood the hood
with drool or spluge
she'll smile at us like Cat Ballou,
        flap her gals, purse her lips,
spin on her heels and shoot from her hips!
        "I'm your huckleberry!"
Oh, Annie Fanny Oakley, we've not seen the last of them!
The girls will have their spills!
'Cause when the dough be runnin' out,
Dar's gold in dem dar hills!

Shun the Turn Signal

Michael Harty

You know you always wanted
to feel like an outlaw, outrage
and intimidate those dutiful drones
wanting to keep you between the lines.
So refuse to join that flock
of mechanical sheep, taillights flashing
like metronomes: yes sir, yes sir,
now I'm about to turn, now I'm turning,
now I'm completing my turn.

Who made your ninth-grade teacher
the ultimate authority?
Keep them guessing, make
the other guy stay alert. Flexibility:
leave room to change your mind.
If people have to know your every move,
you've got Facebook. On the road
don't tip your hand, keep them honest.
And be truthful yourself: after all,
can you really claim
to know exactly where you're going?

On Rereading Poe's "The Raven"

Jan D. Hodge

As I thumbed the pages gazing at their convoluted phrasing,
Lines advancing by repeating what had oft been writ before,
I was yawning at the palling author's stuporific crawling
Through a story unenthralling, going nowhere o'er and o'er,
Words redundantly repeated not just once but o'er and o'er,
   Rhetoric and nothing more.

So this guy is sitting, moping, lost in thought and barely coping,
Haunted by his lost Lenore, his lovely, lovely lost Lenore.
I had sought the simple pleasure of an evening's gentle leisure
Reading poems in stately measure—not a turgid, dismal bore
Droning on interminably. What a self-important bore!—
   Merely that and nothing more.

Then Erato to the rescue; pointing at him with a fescue,[1]
His impatient Muse advised him: "Get a Grip,[2] I thee implore."
Spurred on by this timely citing, he took pen in hand, delighting
In a fevered frenzy, writing as he hadn't heretofore,
Dramatizing now his burden as he couldn't heretofore:
   "Quoth the raven, 'Nevermore!'"

Ah, there's yet another stanza (Pardon; make it *nine;* the man's a
Paragon of persiflage, a babbling, bloviating snore!)
With his assonantal chiming of an acrobatic climbing
To another fitful rhyming on the theme of lost Lenore.
Oh! this mournful, dreary miming of the lovely lost Lenore,
   Lost to him for evermore.

Please, desist! No longer feigning, I, my interest sorely waning,
Lunged and, crumpling up the pages, threw them in the cuspidor,
Then, as verbal corollary, spoke aloud this commentary

To the chill, indifferent air, "Enough!" and resolutely swore—
Cursing the whole of Baltimore, lewdly, eloquently swore—
   To reread it nevermore.

[1] a small pointer used to point out letters to children learning to read [2] Reportedly Poe had originally conceived of his avian visitor as an owl; hence the presence of Pallas [Athena] in the poem. Then, reading Dickens's new novel, *Barnaby Rudge*, he encountered Grip, Barnaby's pet talking raven, and voilà!

At Samson's Ford

Katherine Hoerth

The Samsons of today need pick-up trucks,
not lion-ripping strength or holy strands
of flowing hair (for men, that's kinda queer),
implies the salesman to my husband whose
accountant biceps hint that he could use
a little extra masculinity.

The traffic light turns red and Samson slams
the F150's brakes. The salesman, riding
shotgun at his side, sweet talks the torque,
horsepower and the sparkly rims in chrome.

A KISS song blazes from the radio,
It's Modern Day Delilah, *Same old ways.*
Blondes have more fun! Gene Simmons shrieks. I scoff.

The salesman peeks into the backseat, asks
how true it is – the first and only time
he speaks to me. I grasp a flaxen lock
and twirl it round my finger, might as well
just play along. He smiles, satisfied,
continues speaking in the tongues of man.
And from the corner of my eye, I see
a flash of light and search the intersection
for its sacred origin – the Texas sun
reflecting off a pair of silver bull's
balls, dangling from the truck in front of us.

The traffic light turns green and engines grunt.
I dream of scissors, songs of sharpening
a blade across a whetstone: *Same old ways.*

Eve Finally Makes Adam a Sandwich

Katherine Hoerth

My Adam was a man of simple tastes,
both at the kitchen table and in bed—
baloney with a slice of cheddar cheese,
a beer in hand, and he was satisfied.

The same routine would play out every day:
he'd slap the meat and cheese on plain white bread
then scarf it down, get back to work outside,
as if his food were just for sustenance

and not for pleasure. One day I surprised
him in kitchen, sliced a focaccia roll
in two, slathering each piece with brie,
softened to velvet by the sun. I stacked
the meats, curled them into one another,
a blushing slice of ham, an alabaster
piece of turkey, a bit of roast beef soaked
in merlot. And in the center, I slipped
something special in for him to try—

a gala slice so thin that when you held
it to the window, the sun shone through
like something sacred. I served him with my hands.
I smiled, nodding, knowing it was good.

The Fall of Girl
Katherine Hoerth

While skating down suburban streets,
the hot breeze hit my oily skin.
My teenaged mind was cumulous
and filled with daydreams: boys who played
guitar, drove rusty pickup trucks,
threw football every Friday night.
I sliced into the pavement, turned
the corner, heard a whistle from
behind, and then a voice call out:

Hey pretty gal, slow down let
Us get a better look at you.

You're not supposed to turn around
As if all catcalls were for you.
I peeked over my shoulder, saw
Behind me there were three young men
with goofy smiles, one wore a wife
beater, another had a 'stache

Hey pretty gal! How old are you?

His words like hungry fingertips
that test the ripeness of a peach.
I sneered. I turned my back and raised
my fist up to the sky, outstretched
my middle finger high. I thought
their jeers would echo through the street.
Instead, I only heard the lilts
of mockingbirds. A wicked grin
slashed into my guileless face.
I picked up speed and took a turn
too fast. My balance lost, I fell
and tumbled to the asphalt ground.

But I remember looking back,
relieved to find no one had seen
my nasty fall from grace, relieved
to know the hands of men weren't what
I needed to rise up again.

celebrity chef
Lynn Hoffman

your cooking, man
every dish,
every saucy pro-duckshun
each plagiaralitistic pluctation—
is a route to get around
the downtown bound
train of you having
no native taste at all.
your cooking, man,
is about laying out
a split-open peach
and hoping that
the flies decide
to land.

well yeah, i built that dish
from rumor and tuber
there really wasn't
a muse in my mise so
i fired up the random recipe engine
and sometimes that cooked me good
and well, browned.
and the customers slapped
slapped the table.
and you, tv boy?
you blame me?

Honeymoon
Sally Houtman

Worn thin by apologies
too numerous to name,
the young bride packed light,
stood waiting, as directed,

backlit in the doorway—
in her heavy suitcase
a silver key, one pair of shoes
and her father's gun.

Conference Room Chairs
Ann Howells

Like ants in a hill,
or grackles on a wire,
each perfectly duplicates every other.
Sturdy. Serviceable. Lightweight.
Unobtrusive as only drab grey can be,
they stand at attention in unbroken rows,
molded plastic, better suited
to stacked storage than comfortable seating.
Their saving grace? A tendency
to numb buttocks, make an audience squirm
enough to caution all but the most loquacious
and egotistical speaker to adhere strictly
to his assigned time slot.

Queasy Rider

Ann Howells

Stuck in traffic at LBJ and Preston,
I suck down exhaust, gasoline and burning rubber,
hear my gelatinous lungs make a muckety-muckety
sound like oil-gummed valves,
rue the day I learned: *All smells are particulate.*
I studiously avoid a roadkill raccoon
whose rot pungently wafts the alley,
inhale secondhand smoke in a bar under duress
and without murdering the son-of-a-bitch
who blows it in my face, cringe as a neighbor
lifts the snap-on lid to sniff suspiciously
a tidbit from her refrigerator, *This safe-to-eat?*
But, most importantly, I've learned:
never enter the restroom following a good-ole-boy
who exits hitching his jeans.

Baywatch
Andrew Hudgins

Jiggery-pokery,
Pamela Anderson's
chemistry's wonderwork,
shaped to exalt

polyelectrolyte
gels made of chitosan,
glutamic acid and
aqueous salts.

Hollywood Dreams

Andrew Hudgins

Tittity, tattity,
Fredericks of Hollywood,
vendor of sleaze for us
cheaply debauched,

sold us our sexual
armamentarium—
ersatz silk underpants,
crotchless and crotched.

A Self-Made Man

Marc Jampole

What I coulda been, what I shoulda done,
he speculates in peculated hyperspace
while waiting for his logged-on self to form.
Now I get everything I want and right away in cyberspace,

My avatars jet skis at Tahoe,
climb up walls at Jackson Hole,
motorbike Kahoolawae,

He's posing with his posse,
chilling with the Chili Peppers,
onstage with Alan Jackson fondling chorines,
buying icon tambourines as souvenirs of best-of-times.

I am that I am, he exclaims in pixilated self-perfection,
while switching screens to check his email.

Adding up his passwords, avatars and handles,
he has more names than Arjuna,
more faces than a kabalistic god,
multiple windows of worlds,
and the permanence of love, his online wife,
more cuddly than *that bitch who's bugging me*
to fix the dripping bathroom sink.

Re-Enactment Lawn Service

Mark Allen Jenkins

The ad said, "See history in your own front yard."
I admit, I am skeptical
when General Lee drives up
on his riding mower, Traveler.
When I ask the general about his profession,
he says, "It is good that yard work is so terrible,
lest we grow too fond of it."
When he addresses an entire gray regiment
from his gray mount, I try not to watch.
He reminds them of the constant struggle
against growth, leaves yellowing,
and the importance of vigilance against both.
They quickly rake leaves into ruthless order.
The leaves are stacked against a fence,
when several dozen men in blue march
up the road. Their leader, General Sherman,
chewing on a cigar, starts a gas-powered leaf blower,
shouts, "Leave no leaf unburned."

A strange conflict erupts:
men meeting each other between bare trees
some rolling in leaf piles, rakes clanking.
I see men beaten with handles and slowly
the spades come out, a hand is severed,
and the red maple leaves spread out again.
As the Confederates retreat, I hear Lee yell,
"If only Stonewall Jackson were here,
to mulch these Yanks away!"
I want them to go, to leave me alone and rakeless,
I must stand before red, white, and blue banners,
adjust my black stove pipe hat and beard,
address the crowd of hoop-skirted women,
and read "With malice towards none."

Mosquito

William Jones

I think I could make peace with a mosquito
If she'd just take a bit of my blood and go about her business.
I mean, I have Buddhist proclivities, don't like killing anything,
And if the damn mosquito would just take a dainty sip and move on,
I'd say, go in peace, little sister, living's a hard road for all us,
Take what you need and go.

But the greedy little bitch always comes back for more. Always.
And so at some point, itching all over my ankles and wrists and neck,
I'll start lying in wait for the little sucker,
And if I'm luckier than she is:
SPLAT!
I'll crush her dead, make her little more than a dirty, bloody stain on my
      leg or arm,
Contemplate once again how much capitalism and mosquitoes have in
      common.

What I Learned in Boy Scouts

William Jones

Well, there was the time the scout from Spain
Told us how to fuck a cat
Giving us a visual as his hands
Pretended to hold two back legs
As he pulled the yowling creature
Onto his stiff adolescent prick.

Or the time the scout from England
Showed us what an uncircumcised penis looked like,
Its hooded glory in marked contrast to our German helmets.

Or the dirty jokes told around the campfire
Late at night after the adults had gone to bed,
With punchlines like, "Ding-dong, dammit. Ding-dong," and "Shh! They 'bout to land."

Or how to put a fire out by pissing on it,
Giant white plume rising into the night sky,
Smell of ammoniac embers burning the nose,
Strange disinclination to cook over said fire the morning after.

But also how to build a fire with no more than two matches,
How to tie knots like an old-time sailor,
How to lash poles together to build towers,
And, at least in theory, a bridge.
How to put up and break down camp,
How to pack forty pounds in a pack
And carry it entire days,
Living, mostly, on only what you can carry on your back.

Or canoeing for days down a filthy river
With nasty white foam washing off of the farm fields we passed
Ensuring we paddled our canoes carefully
So as not to end up next to it.

Or how to sleep under a billion stars,
The shy Milky Way standing out clearly
To my eyes away from city lights for the first time.

Or the total silence of a forest night with no human noise
Except the tiny bit we brought.

Buzzing Fly
Steven G. Kellman

I heard a fly buzz when I died—
It broke the peace and hurt my pride.
The hateful seamstress—Refuse to tip her!
Left me—with a noisy zipper.

The Roads All Taken

Steven G. Kellman

Two roads diverged in a wood, and I
Took both, which is why
There are no roads left in the yellow wood,
Which, for the health of sylvan growth,
Is for the good, is for the good.

My Last Boyfriend
Jennifer Kidney

homage to "My Last Duchess" by Robert Browning

Here's the Facebook Profile
of my last boyfriend.
Notice the floppy hat
pushed down to the tops of his ears,
the brim barely revealing
his warm hazel gaze.
See his engaging grin.
He'd cast that delighted smile
on anyone who'd listen
to his elaborate fish tales.
Behold the glittering fish
stretched across his massive chest
held up at both ends like a trophy.
He later threw it back.
I'd been wishing
for bass for dinner, alas.
I gave him copies of my books.
He'd read the poems,
making their stories his own,
forgetting where they came from.
Then he'd wax poetic
about the latest Robert Ludlum.
And he continued to accept
Friend Requests
from younger and younger women.
So I executed commands
and I unfriended him.
He's still clueless.
Let's close this page
and shut down the computer.
Come into the living room.
Notice this delicate watercolor
of a scissortailed flycatcher
painted just for me
by my boyfriend before the last.
Now that, my friend, was love.

Misanthrope

Cindy King

I hate the sound of the human voice
as it bursts from the radio
at sunrise, when yellow holds its breath

and pretends again to be orange.
Daybreak: blood in the palm of morning,
prison-soap pink spills on the horizon
in the so-what of dawn.

I hate the sight of the human form
casting shadows on the grass at midday,
when sky blue becomes handicap in the anti-
freeze of the green afternoon. Full sun
streams caution tape in the what-difference-
does-it-make of day.

I hate the scent of the human body
as it sweats in the subway. Earwax
of the setting sun, sunlight shines
through a prescription bottle
in the whatever of evening.

I hate the touch of the human hand
as it bids farewell. The suffocation
blue of sunset, when the moon rises
like grease cooling in a cast iron skillet
in the never-mind of twilight.

I hate the taste of the human heart
rising bitterly in my throat. Dusk,
a spike of black ice
growing from a stovepipe,
darkness, the dead eye of the stove.

In the biting, wordless, get-on-with-it of night,

                                                            love me.

Narc Anon

Cindy King

Hi, my name is _____, and I am a recovering narcissist.
Yes, I drink, but only to see my face
as it appears grinning, again and again
at the bottom of my glass.
I eat, yes, but only to check my image,
however small, smiling in the curve of the spoon.
Yes, I sleep, but only to impress the mattress.
It has been hard, always being the smartest
person in the room, evading boredom by sketching
my portrait, dreaming up pennames
under which to self-publish my biography.
Yes, I talk to myself with a parrot's shame,
which is to say with none at all,
peck affectionately at my own reflection.
Yes, I have killed my father,
with too much love and acupuncture, and my
mother when she tried to force me
back into her body. My child self has spoken
to the adult. I have learned
the names of my ancestors. Yes, Jesus loves me.

Here's to shooting the wounded and sucking
all the air from the room. To thinning the pack,
and to isolating the weak from the herd.

Here's to the tears in my lashes
that make them shine like black vinyl
and play to my audience like a sentimental recording.

Here's to my heart, limping
on crutches, rattling like the cup of a beggar.
To the fact that I am afraid
that if I stop talking, I may forget to breathe.

Here's to when I tried to kill myself,
to no one stopping me, to all the would-be suicides
who leap from second-story windows.

Kitchen

James Henry Knippen

Pineapple lychee hibiscus rooibos Republic
of Tea. Capresso espresso. Ten cup

capacity. A simple mojito or mango martini.
Belvedere Grey Goose Imperia Wine Monkey.

Merlot cabernet sauvignon chardonnay
and pinot noir in that order for sake

of this song not becoming too drunk
on itself. Clatter of anapest; life of a shelf.

Rhythm of kitchens collapsing on kitchens.
We cut into this counter; it refuses to bleed.

A jam in the garbage disposal establishes
a frying pan's buoyancy, sink-water's

canvass-like properties. We'd like to thank
gravy for making this possible. Ham hocks

for having this happen. Please excuse us.
We know that horseradish hazelnut hummus

sounding so right is so wrong. This banquet's
been made a thousand times over. Our goose

has been cooked in black garlic and butter.
Our goose is refuse. Your goose is still raw.

Fly

Joe R. Lansdale

There is a fly upon the wall
I pulled its wings off,
but still it crawls,
I stuck a pin right through its head
Hard to believe but it ain't dead
I lit a match to its ass
Okay, that did it.

Hussies Don't Wear Girdles, Girls
John B. Lee

for Dorothy Lee Kay

Stella warned her daughters
"always wear your girdles
respectable and modest women
worry about the flesh
that jiggles"—
and "hussies don't wear girdles, girls"
she added—
still, her eldest daughter Mary married badly
a bride in trouble
at the altar, she gave birth
a few months short of nine months wed
after leaving the farm
and then the years unfolding sadly she
abandoned her twelve-year-old child
leaving her to fend for herself alone in an apartment
in the big city

Mary became the wild wife
chasing her man
a butcher's apprentice
a nogoodnik
hard drinker, bad seed
with an eye for the ladies
and he left her alone in the night
her spirit cracked
like hard clay in a dry wind until
she took her own life
and thereby entered
the long and soothing lie of family lore
for everyone said she died of a weak heart

and if we laugh to think of the foolish passions
of the past, or if we fail to feel
the bone-cold winters that sometimes come
to the soul of youth

we too might wish to gird the body
with a better darkness
and the mind with a warmer light

Dedication
Wayne Lee

—for my beloved wife and life partner Chastity, who has always—well, sometimes—been there for me when I needed her most; who has so often inspired me, as well as the personal trainers with whom she's had multiple indiscreet affairs over the past twenty-three years; whose passion and joie-de-vivre have always given me great satisfaction and, on several occasions, sexually transmitted diseases; whose ever-cheerful demeanor has been expertly maintained through long-term psychiatric assistance and the latest pharmaceutical advances, and whose physical beauty has been enhanced and prolonged by eleven different cosmetic surgeries; who feathered our seven-bedroom adobe nest with rare and exotic artifacts we not only couldn't afford but which drove us into bankruptcy and ultimately foreclosure; whose creative accounting practices doomed my company and subjected me to extensive fines, fees and federal prison time; whose athletic prowess was evident as she stood naked, shouldering her designer Glock with perfect posture and textbook technique during our recent armed confrontation while the tantric yoga instructor cowered under the circular vibrating bed; and who shall always be my one true love, even as she writhes relentlessly in the fiery furnace of the blackest bowels of eternal Hell.

The HOA Lady and Her Dog
Michael Mark

They come as a committee, she and her dog.
They pick at our flowers and house paint colors,
appraising the degree of fadedness,
and count weeds, measure lawn color and grade
neatness of curb sweeping.

We hate her, naturally, and wish her and her family
bad things.
Such things that appear in the anemic community paper
that sneaks up on our garage doors, our dented garage doors,
but nothing that would make the headlines, not that bad.

And not anything to harm her dog either.
Her older golden seems sweet and to know
the situation and feel shame, as they walk the neighborhood.

The bright yellow plastic poop bag, a flag, hangs
from the HOA lady's pocket
enough to make the statement that she does the right thing,
armed with her notepad and favorite headband
with the fish design of Jesus,
pink on most days, but she will wear the baby blue
a fair share of the time.

Judgment is her natural gift.
In the way the professional athlete knows
where the ball will be before it is struck,
she has the absolute knowledge of how much
underbrush is acceptable.
This is what the certified letter we received stated, twice –
that we had unsightly and excessive "underbrush" and
there would be "a lien placed on our home
should it not be attended to promptly."

She was elected by the Homeowners Association Executive
Committee without a vote.
No one would think to contest her.
Not her of knees whitened from being pressed
so tightly together when she sits in discussion circles,
waits at stop signs to the count of six,
and when she lies in bed with her husband
who is also a judger,
at the Little League, a decider of strikes and balls
and who is safe and who is out at all the playing fields
from here to the next neighborhood.

I'll admit my garden is likely better kept for her monitoring.
And though I protest to my wife and kids, I have no deep feelings
for the weeds who have died at her whim.
I can also see the uniformity of the houses is comforting
during these challenging times, if not confusing on buzzy weekend
nights returning from some friendly drinking.
We all have pulled into the driveway of an identical replica
of our home sweet home.

During the holidays, I see her in her reindeer sweater,
antlers on her dog, and sense some admiration
as she counts the number of Christmas lights
strung on each house, standing on her toes
to take in the roofs and chimneys,
calculating their level of brightness and potential infractions.

It is no secret that her dogs are barkers.
And I would have to believe this causes her great emotional
and physical pain,
keeping her up nights and her medicine cabinet, neatly filled
with Zantac.
It is a matter of public record,
as the incidences have been reported by the neighbors
for the regular pre-dawn disturbances. Sundays they seem most active –
and that is, of course, the worst day,
the Lord's day, the Sabbath, but she tells
her church friends and their priest that her
babies see the Messiah coming back and that is the reason,
though that is not how she can respond in her written reports
to the complaints or she would risk ridicule
among the non-believers.

She just apologizes and promises to make changes and threatens
the dogs when her husband is out of the house that they will be
replaced by a quieter breed.
She would always have dogs, though, at least two.
When you are on the Homeowner's Association Landscaping Committee,
when you *are* the committee, you need protection.

I know her route and her times.
And when I see her turn in to our cul-de-sac
I take out my most vicious-looking, rusted,
gardening tool.
I put on my wicker sun hat and canvas gloves
and go outside and lift the long pole up high,
like Moses did with the Tablets
and come down hard,
the sharp edge breaking into the ground,

frightening the petunias and other discount annuals.
It is meant to show the HOA committee chair
I am dutifully following, being a good citizen—
and to scare the shit out of her.

She walks her old girl across the street for safety,
and to examine the Chinese neighbor's shedding tree,
counting the leaves on the grass, shrubs, the sidewalk,
the curb, checking off boxes and then to turn and get another
perspective on my house and my vegetable garden that I know,
 the whole neighborhood knows, she has her eye out for.
And that is why earlier I removed my underwear and belt.
So when I bend over in my jeans,
for according to the HOA bylaws there is no officially required
gardening dress code,
the sweaty material grabs my thighs
and pulls lower for her to see,
as I dig out some fresh unsightly underbrush
before it makes her notes.

The Last Laugh
Michael Mark

Dealing with insurance
companies sucks
the trust right out of me.

"Please stop the jargon,"
I tell the helpline lady
who uses the name Gail,
"and slow down for the old man."

She apologizes and asks me to verify
my social security number
and account information.

Then she apologizes again for the wait
while she researches the reason my policy
has been cancelled.

In the pause, I know
I am cancelled.

As I am at restaurants.

They get me out of the way
before the
two and three beer
and appetizer orderers
take over,

slap the check down
with my "senior slice" of pie

and pass right by my empty cup,
the coffee pot hot in their hands.

Gail comes back on the phone happy.
She says she gets the last laugh

because she checked and
found out that she's older than me.

Of course, that's the big prize, isn't it?
To get the last laugh.

And the ones who always do
are the insurance companies.

It's their business.

To Be a Gringo in Mexico

David Michael Martinez

*. . . I think that a pretty good way to depart this life. It beats old age,
disease, or falling down the cellar stairs.*

—Ambrose Bierce

More than a man was lost
when Ambrose Bierce rode south
into the Mexican Revolution.

The old gringo with Villa's army
rode in Chihuahua and Tierra Blanca
embroiling skulking Federales
who returned the septuagenarian's
Aquí está su padre, cabrones
with fervent percussions of lead.

If the Mexicans shot him anywhere
it was in the mouth—*sí señor*,
another loud-mouthed gringo
in an unmarked grave.

Altogether, All Together

Janet McCann

I liked nude not naked, the smoother
skin. Nudist camps were beautiful bodies draped
on the beach as in Seurat's painting, but without clothes.
Naked was warts and freckles
and a hand slapping a bum. Naked was
bright sunlit nasty revelation, nude was
more dawn or dusky. I swam nude in the club
pool, it was almost dark, my friends swam with me.
Mosquitos bite naked people, we were immune.
When the lights went on in the club, we
found that we were naked and we ran,
leaving bras and panties on the fence.

Do you go to bed nude and wake up naked?
What about unclothed? That is a mannequin
in a store, or maybe someone stepping into a
shower. The model is undraped, not unclothed.
Jaybirds do not wear clothes but they aren't
naked either. My student wrote that she liked to dine
au naturel with her family and friends
but she meant al fresco. My college friends and I
played strip poker on the train but did not
disrobe entirely, the first to chicken out
bought us all drinks. What fun it was
to walk up to the bar in a shift, order beer.

Girly Restaurant in Texas

Janet McCann

Leaves from the plant store
invade the patio,
grapple the bentwood chairs.
The menu is almost all quiche
and salad, I have a tiny
chicken breast glazed with
cranberries. So many women
outside, inside, buying begonias,
lobelias and little pots of
herbs for the kitchen garden, women
fumbling the wind chimes, checking
their makeup in the wrought-iron
framed mirrors. Artificial cats
in apparent sleep dot the benches,
you have to touch one
to see she isn't real. I want a man
to shove his way in here
with a big golden retriever.
I want the dog to gobble up
the fake cats, the man to
holler for a Lone Star.
I want the waitresses
in their green elf suits to run like hell.

In a Bar

Janet McCann

at the celebration of Emily Dickinson's 177th birthday

You are reading intensely, underscoring
the key words, that one verb
you hunted half the night for, looking up
at the West Texas stars, when
a woman walks through your poem.
Glittery red sweater, high-heeled boots,
she stalks negligently across the floor,
shows us her sleek denim butt
as she clacks over the wooden boards,
up the ramp and out into the back.
You slow down your reading, miss
a comma, then pick it up again
and continue. But the poem's changed.
Now it has her footsteps in it.
You will always slow at just that point
in vague puzzlement, hearing them,
and when it comes out in *Chelsea Review*
readers will look at it twice and they will say,
it's all about a West Texas landscape
but there seems to be a woman in it.

St. Joseph's Day (Independence, La.)

Jerry McElveen

Oh, God, here they come again. Every year
it's the same old routine. Eight paunchy,
hairy-eared, one-eyebrowed, squat old Dagos
showing up to haul me out of the church and through the streets.
They'll take me off my pedestal here in Mater Dolorosa,
hoist me up on a bier, drape me with garlands
of sewn-together U.S. currency, and up we go.
They'll ride me on their shoulders like Cleopatra
coming to Cairo. But the train depot here in Little Italy
ain't exactly the pyramids, you know?
And that fingernail-scraping-on-a-chalkboard voiced little priest
will drive me nuts again with his Hail Marys
from that sound truck at the head of the parade.
And how come it's always "Hail Marys" anyhow?
How about "Hail Josephs" for a change? I mean,
it's not as if I wasn't there, too, you know.
Well, here we go—up, up, and away. Lord a mercy!
This so-called "Town Band" is one sorry-ass excuse
for a bunch of musicians. But compared to their marching skills,
they sound like the U.S. Marine Band. Maybe it'll rain
and we can call this thing off early. Wouldn't want
to get my halo wet. Uh-oh, wait a minute. We didn't get far
before some sinning strawberry-farmer spectator decided
he wanted a picture of me in exchange for a "donation"
to the church. Wouldn't surprise me if
Father Delta Pinto, or whatever his name is, claimed
I had autographed each one personally. Easy, Boys,
don't drop me. I'm pretty fragile, you know. OK, then,
stitch that ten-spot to the rest and let's get going.
My God, look at those nuns, would you?
Don't good-looking women ever take vows? Talk about scary!
Sister Mary Birddog and Sister Theresa Mastiff raise
ugliness to new heights. And these sweet altar boys,
wearing their white gowns and carrying their staffs—
I'm a little nervous about the way Father DP
looks at them, if you get my drift.
Dang, it's hot and muggy today. It's enough
to make a statue sweat! Sure as I do, though, one of these
religious freaks will claim she saw me crying
and pronounce it a miracle, some kind of sign from God!
Lord, I hate zealots, especially the religious variety.
Oh boy, here come the garlic-smelling grandmas,
their shoes in one hand and their rosaries in the other.
I guess they think that tearing up their stockings
and their feet on these gravel streets will draw them

closer to God or something. Wonder why the men
don't shuffle their fat asses around the town
in their sock feet? Might take a few thousand years off
their Purgatory sentence. Steady now, Paisanos! The main
Street is pretty steep! Wouldn't look too good in the headlines
of the *Independent* if you let me tip off this little platform,
now, would it? I can see it now: "Local Catholics Dump
Saint Joseph." The Pope would be plenty pissed, let me tell you.
Ah, now we're back on level ground, and I can soon get
some peace and quiet back at the church. I can hardly wait.
All this pomp and parading really wears me out.
That's it; unlace these money streamers from around my neck
and set me back on my pedestal for another year.
Whoa, what's this? Dominick and Angelo stuffing a couple
of twenties in their pockets? Mother of God, some people
will steal from even a saint—like me.
All right, Goombahs, you did a good job. Now get on over
to the Rec Center and grab those Bingo cards and beer.
By this time tomorrow, you'll only remember the dancing
and the fireworks anyhow, not anything about old St. Joe
and his contributions. But don't worry about it.
I'm used to being ignored. Even Mary forgot all about me
once Jesus turned twelve.

So We Painted It Red
Bryce Milligan

So we painted
it red

left it in
the rain

and waited there
for God

to send white
chickens

Continuing On to a Final Destination: Contemporary Air Travel in 3-D

John Graves Morris

"In preparation for landing,"
the flight attendant utters by rote
so lockstep she does not even need
to think. She clicks the microphone

off to stifle a yawn and recites,
"please be sure to return seats
to their upright and locked position."
She must see those seats in her dreams.

First-class passengers earlier strolled
a lane fashioned out of air, jerryrigged
with iron standards and elastic tape
above a moveable bright red carpet

already starting to show signs of wear,
the imagery and puffery of an illusory
extra lane of service, issued
by employees like pairs of 3-D glasses,

another combination of hype and hardware
designed to provide less for more
because, as the marketers say to
bean counters, "there's a sap for that."

Coach fliers, who checked in on a computer
to save the cost of employees, were invited
to "upgrade" their seats to "Economy Plus"
for an additional $65 for the leg room

that used to be provided free in exit rows.
Checking a bag now costs $25, and passengers
who wanted to pay cash were invited to another
line to pay it. They then hurried up to wait

until the spokesperson, who tagged baggage,
loaded the plane, and worked security, said
"at this time," never *now*, "we begin our
boarding process." After a late departure,

after passengers have been cramped in rows
in which their knees were crushed against
the reclined seats in front of them,
after they have starved unless they paid more,

after the plane has bumped down and bled speed,
the attendant intones, "Welcome to Los Angeles/
Boston/Detroit/Atlanta. You may retrieve
your bags from carousel four. For those

continuing on, please check the monitor.
From your New York/Dallas/Salt Lake City-
based crew, welcome home here to Chicago
or wherever your final destination takes you."

The Hospital Administrator's Wife
karla k. morton

Looking around, she realizes
every man at this table
has fingered her vagina,

or seen the drop of her unconscious jaw,
or probed her anus and upper colon,
or felt her breast
and squeezed her nipples.

And she looks at her husband—
clueless of her strength—
who's never once admired
how well she makes small talk;
smiling over coffee and cake.

Beach Scene
Tom Murphy

Too bad,
I was all ready to go buy
a shotgun to randomly
to shoot off while we ran our
flag wrapped bodies like
bacon around sirloin
down the beach after the
bouncing boobs as they
scream running in their
backward bug-eyed
sunglass and tie bottom
bikinis just to covet their
discarded beer stuffed
coolers and their "clit lit"
trade papers to toss on the
bonfire as slam-dance the
flames in a brew frenzy
romp-o-rama.

Too bad,
I wasn't invited.

Forecast

Laurence Musgrove

There remains a great deal
Of uncertainty about me
During the next few hours,
Over the course of the evening,
And up until and through
The coming weekend.

Even the slightest change
In my activity or schedule
May make a significant
Difference in the number
And kind of future actions
You may see me undertake.

So I encourage everyone
To continue monitoring
My developing situation
And to take whatever
Precautions necessary
Until you hear the "all clear."

Somebody
Laurence Musgrove

At my house I'm really Somebody.
Somebody needs to empty the garbage.
Did Somebody bring the mail in?
Looks like Somebody tracked this dirt in.
If Somebody could come help me.
Did Somebody take the dogs for a walk?
Somebody left a mess in here.
Somebody should call a plumber.
Somebody forgot to lock the door again.
Somebody needs to run to the store.
I hope Somebody left a light on.
Somebody will thank me later.
Yes, I'm Somebody all right.

Dream the Illiterate Dream or Don't Dream At All

Dave Newman

She says "What are you going to do
now that you don't have a job?"

and I say "Collect unemployment
and write novels about Pittsburgh"

and she says "That's stupid."
She says "You should write porn."

To the Woman in the Grocery Line Who Complains
about the Man in Front of Us because He Wears Nike
Shoes and Pays for His Groceries with Food Stamps
 Dave Newman

It's possible that he
        like many
        intelligent consumers
bought the shoes on sale.

Two Kinds of Minds

Chris O'Carroll

Do women talk three times as much as men?
This book—it's by a woman shrink—says yes.
Would a male writer say the same, or would
He somehow manage to say two-thirds less?

Men's brains, the book says, spark with thoughts of sex
Once every minute; women's brains do not.
I don't know if the author's right or wrong,
But who cares? Let her talk. She's pretty hot.

The Frank Gaze of Women

Dave Parsons

after Baudelaire's "Exotic Scent,"

   to W. C. Williams & all those anthologists

Yes, yes, they bestow delights—
　　　not only in the seedy way
we all know: they plant something
　　　in the littoral vacancy
and in an instant there is an ineffable
　　　fire—that forging force
on which so much more depends
　　　than wheelbarrows & chickens

You Fold This Sweater
Simon Perchik

You fold this sweater the way a moth
builds halls from the darkness it needs
to go on living—safe inside this coffin

a family is gathering for dinner, cashmere
with oil, some garlic, a little salt, lit
and wings warmed by mealtime stories

about flying at night into small fires
grazing on the somewhere that became
the out-of-tune hum older than falling

– you close this closet draw and slowly
your eyes shut – with both hands
make a sign in the air as if death matters.

Southern Customs
George Perreault

Some places they
cut parts out of people and
toss them into the street.

Some places they
hand you
the knife.

Carmen Miranda, They're Going To Bag Your Bananas in Plastic but I Love Them Still

Walt Peterson

I wann'a be your Banana Boat Belafonte,
Goddess of aisle 1,
you shine a golden nimbus in my Giant Eagle.
Let's tango from this cabbage madness,

forget "de deadly black tarantula,"
machete our way through heads of lettuce,
supermarket managers, florets of broccoli
to find who's covered your regal gold
with plastic bags:

Oh, heinous sin against Mother Nature's answer
    to the snap-top,
flip-top, zipper, button, steering wheel club,
hinged coffin lid.

You grow your own,
keep your underwear clean,
carry your house, wrapper, shell, vacuum
sealed container on your back.
How I dream to undress you,
peel your silk, sleek skin.

Now, my Sweets,
the nefarious Pacific Fruit Company surrounds you with polyethylene dreams.
Next, each of your cute fruits gets a condocondom jumpsuit.
Mark what Tarzan said,
"Remember the banana:
once it leaves the bunch
it gets skinned!"

You are my cream-dream
on Rice-Chex with milk,
even in the buff, Bonita Chiquita.
Come to me,
Nature's slippery joke—
let's cruise on the breeze of this Bossa Nova.
Aye, potassium Princess,
strip those United Fruit Stickers, blue and yellow,
from your skin to festoon your love letters
then seal them with a kiss.

How I pray to behold
your starches turning to sugar,
gold blushing brown and Latin
in my hot little hunky hands.

Euterpe Laces 'Em Up
Walt Peterson

Coach never claimed he knew poetry
but he taught us

      box & one

            jump-stop at the elbow

    Red thirty-two!

We wore grooves in that damn wooden floor
running his plays.

He's pissed big-time after the tournament game, though,
& smokes me like one of his cheap cigars.
You couldn't hit the broadside of a barn with a
handful of buckshot . . .

So I took the hint,
made the move on to poetry.

Nights now, she comes,
The Muse,
whispers to me—
or a bull's ass with a spade.

Poem with Big Feet
Richard Pflum

This is the poem that walks
on big feet, that stomps on
all smaller poems, that says,
"get out of my way," when it
saunters through the barroom door.
This is the poem that interrupts
the conversation you are having with
your girlfriend and talks her into
dancing and then leaving without you,
so you must go home or dance by yourself.
This is the same poem which sits down
beside you the next day and eats all of
your French fries and wants a big bite
from your cheeseburger. That gives you
free advice about your terminal inadequacies
and offers you a gun, though it admits,
"this is the coward's way out."
This is also the poem which tells you
that any greatness you might achieve
in this world is due to it, while
all failures are strictly your own.

This is the poem which is always
suffering because no one appreciates
its true merit, a poem that knows it
could have been a millionaire or an
important politician had it chosen
to be something else.

This is the poem you avoid trying
to write though it's always around
beating its chest, complaining;
intimidating the lyrical, quieter,
often deeper poems.

Still, because its feet are so big
and its space requirements, enormous,
perhaps it can't help stomping on other
poems and things. Perhaps it is
not even cruel, just deprived;
having grown up without lessons
on the cello, and never enough
cheeseburgers on the backyard patio.

My Friend Told Me
Ken Pobo

that she had been married to
a golf ball
for a dozen years. I tried to picture

dinner at their house. Even
a high chair couldn't help him eat.
A bossy golf ball, he gave her
orders which she followed
while he looked for a hole
in one. When he found that,

he stopped coming home. They
had a "beautiful" house with antiques
and pictures of Arnold Palmer
on the walls. Unloading
all that pretty junk
took months. Some of it
she couldn't part with,

though seeing the golf ball
shoot over the green
and out of sight,
that was joy.

Shucks

Ken Pobo

My wife Raylene says, "You're the type who'd forgive me
if I stepped out on you." I say shucks and tell her I love her
even more than our dog Wizard. She cries
wet atomic warheads. They explode
on our anniversaries. Or messy weather.

I prefer fishing and tell Raylene, "Baby, I'll miss you so bad."
She puts her arms around me, squeezes my ass,
and waves as my pick-up heads for the Delmarva.

Speaking of pick-ups, that's the real reason
I head to eastern Maryland. I chow down
on some women, if I can get them.

One got nasty and I shot her in the face.
She never told. In fact, she asked to see me again.
I said no. I was married. She understood.

I tell Raylene when I get home how nothing was biting.
She heats up those Gorton fish sticks
which we eat with *Family Feud,*
a good lead-in to sex. Sometimes
that gets kind of nuclear. Afterwards,

we feel vaporized, disappeared yet fully present.

The Wisdom Of. The American People.
Ken Pobo

So the great American people
who must be told 24/7 that they are
exceptional,
that they are just a little
more marvelous than everyone else,
support torture,
the religious ones supporting it
more than the rest.

Who would Jesus torture?
Who would Jesus waterboard?

Picture these same people
trapped in some rancid Guantanamo,
begging for breath,
freezing in nasty positions,
guards pissing on their Bibles.

Even then they would say,
"My, my, I'm exceptional."
Even then they'd say,
"Believe John 3:16. Kill them."

Birthday

Leslie Provence

What am I giving your father?

All I could possibly give him

is a clue.

But he is

not

taking

delivery.

What kind of bitch are you?
Leslie Provence

I wasn't raised
to be a bitch
about money.
Or things.

I was raised
to be a bitch
about injustice.
And insult.

Being a bitch
about stupidity?
That was *my* idea.

Being a bitch to someone
who was just trying
to be nice to me?
No idea.

The Father Poet

Mike Pulley

Let's call him the Father Poet.
Having just published his masterpiece of memory,
He arrived in our area at the peak of his powers
With his ear for music of soothing moods.

He drove a deluxe sedan of selfdom
With a sound system of lusciousness
And kept card tricks in his trunk for children
And holy water for the women.

Our daily rag hailed him New Kid in Town
And fastened medals on his breast
And feted him with brunches
And brought him candy.

The students in his class smiled
And tingled inside like loaded addicts
Because they believed his celebrity
Had rubbed off on them.

The way he opened a can of words
Inspired them to try their hand
In the wicked ways
Of rhythmic profit sharing.

"No!" he yelled at them.
He did not want of a cult of imitators,
But a cult of imitators is what he cultivated,
"How the alabaster faces haunted us!"

I guess I was one of the lucky cherubs
Because I was plucked prematurely
From my blackboard of acne and pecking orders
And ushered to his class in the academy.

"You look like my son," he said to me,
And shook my hand with the assurance of a closer,
And I was forever hooked on spooky logic.
I turned to twisting syntax into pretzels.

Soon I was under the wing of his mistress
Making nonsense out of jumbled sequences,
Wondering how I could distinguish myself
With these makeshift meanings.

In the meantime, he continued his climb
With more hardbacks and breakfasts,
Cheese quiches with the chancellor
And makeup for talk show cameras.

The administration overlooked his swilling
And promiscuous use of saturated fats,
Paid no attention to his jailbait lechery,
His preference for sadistic apprenticeships.

He piloted his car like a spaceship
And drunkenly crashed it into the surface of Mars
And even the little green men
Became slaves in his memorization schemes.

His misbehavior merely spurred his puppets
And they pirouetted in his game of roulette,
Served as whirlybirds by dropping leaflets
In praise of his savagery as a form of salvation.

He dispensed advice to his students
Grinning like the Cheshire cat,
And these chosen ones churned out copies
In girdled obedience like eager disciples.

Then all gathered at the gravesite
Ready to praise such profligacy
After the cheating and lying and loving
Brought the drunken bard to early dirt.

More than a decade after his death
I returned to what remained of his wake,
A few faithful congregating in a dream garden
Where I tried to reconnect with old stories.

I was surprised to find his mistress still alive,
For she and others suffered much in his service.
No one seemed bitter and had each other to consider.
Ultimately, his existential lesson prevailed:

The parable of free will in the playground
Where the laws are not enforced
And the imagination is liable only to the sin
Of omission and the poverty of reproduction.

Say, What?
Elizabeth Raby

Only a man
would think
snarky, smart ass
poetry is
something
the world needs
when there is
hardly a civil
word in any
other form
of communication
these days.

Poetry—leaping
into the compost
pile that marks
the disintegration
of civilized
speech.

Oh yes, let's do
make something
worse, something
less than what
came before.

And it's true
I suppose—
eventually worms
make their way
out of the mess,
spur the growth
of some new thing.

A Close Shave
Charles Rammelkamp

"People who shave grow a day younger every morning."
    —Vladimir Nabokov, *Mary*

"You're not supposed to shave in the steamroom."

All lathered up,
feeling my whiskers relax
like moviegoers slumping in their seats,
clutching my razor,
I open my eyes to the muscular young man
hovering over me where I sit on the bench
in the clouds of steam,
a towel swaddled about his waist,
reminding me of the street-crossing guards
in elementary school,
their bright orange vests
their air of faux authority.

"No problem," I lie,
casual as a kid playing hooky,
but feeling like the busted jaywalker,
hurtled back in time half a century.
"I'm just softening my whiskers.
I'll shave out at the washbasins."

"OK, sorry," the kid apologizes,
"It's just that it's against the rules.
Health Department."

As he turns away,
I check the impulse to trip him,
like a sixth-grade bad boy
on the edge of puberty,
anticipating the day
he'll be able to shave like a man.

Prajna

Charles Rammelkamp

In college there were many techniques
to get a girl into your bed.
Some of them worked.

The all-out personality offensive, aka charm;
the poetic, sensitive soul,
sympathetic, caring;
he-man physical animal magnetism;
assertive rock-star self-confidence.

Alex's method was mystic wisdom,
though it took a special girl
to fall for it.

Once at lunch in the cafeteria,
Alex fixed his cobra gaze
on innocent Brenda Mahoney,
stared with Dracula-like intensity
into her eyes.
"Prajna," he murmured, "the Sanskrit term
for wisdom – insight
into the nature of reality:
all is emptiness, *Sunyata.*"

I wanted to laugh,
feeling like I was witnessing a sideshow carnie
in one of those itinerant ramshackle circuses
moving from town to town.

But not ten minutes later,
Alex was leading Brenda by the hand
to his off-campus apartment,
guiding her away like a modern pied piper
with words like *lingam* and *yoni.*

At the cafeteria door, he turned to me
and winked.

A Visit to Merrill Lynch

Carol Coffee Reposa

For this pilgrimage
I wear my best suit
And highest heels,
Arrive on time
Pass quietly
Through glass doors into the temple,
An apotheosis
In granite, chrome, and steel.

My new priest,
Perfect
In black Armani vestments
Escorts me
To the confessional
Where I enumerate
My lapses
And losses.

He calls me to account
On his computer,
Examines my shortfalls
And shortcomings,
Finally absolves me
But only after exacting a penance
Of fees and dollars,
Aves and promises.

After his blessing
I leave by the sleek elevator
And walk out
Into the emerald afternoon,
Its fallen crepes
And roses
Blooming
Hopelessly.

The Fine Print
Marilee Richards

a translation

This medication will not help much,
may not help at all, and there is a good chance
it will make your condition worse or even
create a new and more awful condition
involving the liver, kidneys, spleen, heart, lungs,
or other organs you may have become dependent
upon. Do not take

this medication if you are pregnant,
or may become pregnant,
or have ever been pregnant, or gotten someone else
pregnant, or may be the product of a pregnancy
yourself. If you take

this medication with alcohol, food, while having sex,
reading a good book, gardening, or within
twenty four hours of any activity
you find pleasurable, you will be sorry,

and you may be plucked from the audience
at any time for the purpose of additional fun
being had at your expense. Since

a lot of money and animal experiments
have gone into the creation of this medication,
you will appreciate our desire to serve
your best interests should you ever actually
manage to open this container. A chair

has been placed for your convenience
should you begin to feel dizzy, faint,
or should you fall asleep while operating
heavy equipment, in which case
you should have heeded the warnings
on this label and also consulted
your physician beforehand.

At the Eye Doctor's
Stephen R. Roberts

The doctor asks me to read
the eye chart, line five.
I think it begins with D
but it could be a B or an F.
He asks me if I've had any
problems with my eyes.
I tell him I seem to see
some things a few moments
before they actually happen.
I think he thinks I may be
a soothsayer of some sort,
or an obnoxious space alien
with no applicable insurance.
I can tell he doesn't like me.
He puts chrome and titanium
things onto or near the surface
of my left eye and asks,
how about this form of pain?
He follows it up with, what kind
of advance things have you seen?
I tell him about the break-in
down at the mustard museum
which he hasn't heard about
but it gets us to discussing
the various hues of the condiment.
From there we move on,
discussing the process of smashing
tomatoes into ketchup or catsup
and why there are two ways
of spelling the same thing.
An eyeball, he says, is more delicate
than the finest of tomatoes.
He squirts a fiery substance
into my other eye, then
requests I keep it open
to see what the future brings.

Baked Potato
Stephen R. Roberts

Dear Miss Manners:
Is it polite to eat a baked potato with your hands?

Only if the potato is cool enough
to stand on a street corner,
cigarette dangling,
talking jive potato-trash-talk,
saying, the eyes have it.

Or, if hunger pangs turn so intense
your heart pitter-patters
off your breast-bone improvising
a four-step party-dance
with the tuber of its dreams.

Or, if you believe that eating a potato
in this manner is akin to consuming
oneself in order to comprehend the image
of you as part of the vegetable kingdom
in all its stolid mannerisms and tepid beliefs.

To ask the question, a delicious conundrum
drenched in soy milk and fungal tongues,
stammers around an irreverent quagmire,
the soggy language of your subconscious.

To attempt an answer is a potato waiting
to happen spontaneously, like the tail end
of a dream you grab, expecting to extract it
from the clogged sink-drain of your mind.

Anatomically Correct

Russell Rowland

Of all the dolls I took to bed with me,
she was the most correct,
anatomically.

So real, you could see blue veins
beneath the surface softness of the breasts.
Buttocks goose-bumped in high relief.

Her verisimilitude defied belief.

She mimicked thought;
could say ten words, all synonyms for love—
and must have had

a replica maidenhead like a safety seal,
by the authentic-looking Rorschach on
my bed sheet, which I made her wash.

But when I traded for another doll,
she dribbled from her eyes and nose—
manufacturer's defect, I suppose.

She Was Perfect
Russell Rowland

That little boy barged into the bathroom,
pants already half-unzipped—to recoil
at the burst of light, shower-saturated air,
his bare-naked sister standing there,
her face all eyes and a torrent of words
as she hid behind her arms. The door
slammed, a picture fell, but her afterimage
developed on retentive retinas:
the bouncy things, squished out of sight,
an arrowhead of poodle hair. She was
perfect. His own sister was perfect.

A white string had dangled from her bottom:
this he didn't understand. After school,
he asked Shugrue about it: the big boy
who knew many swears, and the parts of girls;
who paraded in the woods with a BB gun
thrust out between his legs like a weenie.
Shugrue told him the unsettling truth.
All girls have that string. If it gets pulled,
their entire insides fall out.

Quik Stop

Yvette A. Schnoeker-Shorb

Not so when you're quickly stopped
by a bathroom door locked
from the inside. I wait patiently
and pretend to be in the process
of selecting a snack from a rack
as a man in a hurry passes by,
pushes the other door marked *Men*—
resistance there, as well.
He looks at me and questions
the obvious, "Are they both in use?"

For a man who seems in his late thirties,
he is intimately expressive, whispering
"I have to go so bad!" Faking
interest, as I have needs of my own,
I look up to inform him loudly
enough to be heard beyond
locked bathroom doors, "Someone
must be camping in the women's."
He looks even more distressed
by my passive aggressiveness.

"I think it's my kids," he apologizes.
Apart from his use of a singular
pronoun, but as if on cue, both doors
click unlocked and swing open.
Two teenagers who look like him
rush out like darts targeting
the cold drinks aisle as another
woman begins her approach,
but it is my turn, and I've earned
the right to be slow.

Wife Says I Don't Know How To Shut the Door Quietly Prayer

Dustin Scott

Oh great master of the door how your knowledge eludes me
I wish to attain only a glimpse of your greatness
Show me how you master the door oh great one
Bring forth the jewels of wisdom to me
I strive only to be in your shadow as your greatness shines its light on
      the world

The Critic Helps the Poet

Jan Seale

The first 3 lines of this poem
are too prosaic. The second
sentence jerks – tone changes.

DO NOT READ THE ABOVE.

Lines 4-7 show some development
of the idée fixe but
wander too much – thus
chatty and indulgent.

STRIKE LL. 4-7.

Any images coming up are
1) self-serving
2) too easy
3) mannered
4) trivial
5) creaking
6) offensive to my taste.

OMIT ALL QUALIFYING 1) THROUGH 6).

The ending is lame and inept,
sentimental and uncontrolled.

DO NOT END THIS POEM.

P.S. It's a marvelous poem
(tho' not terribly ambitious).

The Pamphlet Lists Ways To Avoid Being a Victim of Rape

Jan Seale

Don't daydream out of doors;
Don't overload your arms;
Don't walk through crowds of men;
Wear a whistle for alarm.

Don't look left or right;
Don't join a crowd for fun;
Don't pause for any reason;
Wear clothes that let you run.

Take as much as several seconds
to analyze and then react
so you do not ride the elevator
with the waiting maniac.

Keep doors and windows locked;
Let no one know you're home:
Put a deadbolt on your door
before you are one.

In conclusion, don't smile,
don't relax, don't play.
Thank you for reading this,
and do have a nice day.

Postcard Wishing You Weren't Here
Jan Seale

A hundred trillion gals. of water backed up
in this lake and I can't remember tonight
which end the dam is damming. Somebody says
3-4 hundred chipmunks in the area all
trained to eat peanuts. Donkey brays on the
½ hr. Fridge and water heater in duet.
Trailside Lodge asks you not to put toilet
paper in the toilet, not to walk your
horse in the septic tank area, not to talk
longer than 3 mins., not to go down the
bank to the water. You may feed the chip-
munks 1 bag 25-cent approved peanuts, fish for
a fee, look at the rental boats, buy
dusty catsup in the Gen. Store. Towels
are changed every third day.

The Feminist Meeting

Allison Sharp

The feminist meeting is always held in the same odd locale.
The room is typically masculine, the attendees are typically not.
The hostess reminds them, "Keep moving past
that floral living room, the kitchen (devilish word)
and on to the den!" Canned beers crack open.
Coors. Keystone. Corona. Never flavored or coolers.
The attendees become cunning and prolific writers.
Drunk, they yell nonsense haikus like

The penises lie
next to the winter fire
while bras turn to ash.

They finish with a midnight vigil under Virginia Woolf's portrait
and map out the extra room they all need
to one day write more than seventeen shrew syllables.

Poems That Continue From

Jon Simmons

the title piss me off poems without
punctuation too
why can't these poets just follow
the rules why do they have to
break
them
there must be a best way to write a poem
these are the same poets ignominious and feared
decried heretics by kings and shackled
serves them right
they shouldn't have ignored basic conventions
they brought it upon themselves
daring to be different

Poems That Continue From

Size Four

Wendy Sloan

to the Lady Invariably Seated on My Left at Lunch

Yeah, right. A salad. Well, I should have known
this place got girls pared down to skin and bone.
Now while I've polished off a full-course meal,
you're still content to munch that lemon peel
hung on your water glass. Take some more sips.
No love handles obscure those skinny hips.
They're sharp as salsa! Girl, you've got some edge.
Splurge on another cut cucumber wedge.
Do I indulge too much? I'm half-way through
dessert, you've taken all that time to chew
up one tomato. Hey, give me a break.
Your vanity is just too hard to take.
Still, I find solace thinking of the dread
your man feels when it's time to climb in bed.

Memento Mori
Loren Smith

When I die,
I want my obituary written in first person.

And since I'm not going to be the one to write it,
because I don't plan on dying anytime soon,
I'd like it to start with something like
"Good riddance world. I've officially transcended hemorrhoids."

And following the circumstances of my death (which should
be an exaggerated lie involving such things as samurai armor and beer)
a filthy little limerick or haiku should appear in it.

Also, please forgo the "loving husband, father, son" routine
because no one says that about themselves
and instead just be blunt which is that
"In '04 I knocked up Jackie" and
"I routinely lied about how much I like stroganoff."

Lastly, I want my obituary to end with what's on my tombstone.
Something like "For god's sake go do something useful,"
or "Damn its hot down here,"
or even something as ominous
as "You're fly's undone," because
that's the obituary that says I'm still alive.

Donkey Show
Tyler Stoddard Smith

Sometimes when
you're with Nathan in Tijuana,
he makes you go to something he calls
a *demostración*, which
he says is like a "cultural surprise"—and it is.
But they
make you order two drinks and
even those don't help;
you feel
so
dirty   after
     ward.

A Long-Suffering Wife Speaks Graveside

Janice D. Soderling

Lately fond of gin and rum,
here lies my household's head
who hid his bottles here and there
and underneath the bed.

Confronted with proof positive
he gaped in mock surprise.
There are no hidden bottles here.
And still he lies.

Elixir of Love

Howard Stein

with apologies to Gaetano Donizetti and gratitude to Helen Fisher

Oh dopamine! Elixir of love!
Beloved catecholamine neurotransmitter,
Child of the hypothalamus—
To you I owe all passion.
In you are all the wiles of Venus,
The drunken orgies of Dionysus.

When I fall in love,
It is you, phantom brew,
Whom I truly cherish.
My beloved in flesh
Is only a stand-in
For the biochemistry between us.

Oh dopamine! Sly Trickster!
You are crueler than Narcissus!
It is not even my self,
But my chemicals,
Whom I most adore.

15 Ways of Looking at a Blackboard
(As it Looks Back)
Bradley R. Strahan

A thousand black birds
Jammed together in the dark—
Petrified feathers

Every Halloween in *the dead of night*
The blackboard factory
Frightens shadows stiff

On the last night of Mardi gras
The New Orleans school board
Invites the King of the Zulus (for a flat fee)

Dracula is bored – goes out
After midnight in his tux
Gets flattened by a Mack truck

This cartoon keeps getting stuck
On *black comedy*
Now jokes are written on Tar Babies

Blackboard in rebellion—
No more chalk dust
Don't mess me simple black dress

Black Beard Black Hole Black Hand—
Too much bad mouth
Wus-a-matter says blackboard

Blackboard protests its reputation
Lighten up whiten up
Chalk it up to experience

Greedy blackboard says to the dark
I've swallowed up all the light
You can't have none

Hungry blackboard wants
Blackened Redfish Black Betty—
Belly full of darkness

Stylish blackboard wants
A red Gucci frame
To be a black Madonna

Filled with admiration
The slate says to blackboard
When I grow up I want to be you

Bombastic blackboard's
Bound to fall—
All those shattering lies

They say the road to hell
Is smooth and slippery—
A blank blackboard

I see the blackboard
And it sees me
Devil take the parson that baptized me

Multiverse

Jeffrey Talmadge

Visible nature is all plasticity and indifference, a moral multiverse, as one might call it, and not a moral universe.

—William James, "Is Life Worth Living?" (1895)

In the alternate universe
everything turned out differently.
The other you has another career,
a house full of loving or bratty kids,
a more or less beautiful spouse.

You exercise every day
and never fail to floss.
You should see your witty self
at parties. Ah, those jokes you tell.
The possibilities, not to mention the realities,
are endless in that parallel life born
of some quantum physicist's theory.

Do you wonder what it would be like
if you'd married your first love,
become a cartographer in Luxembourg,
and told the boss to kiss your ass goodbye?
There's good news.
You did.

Bullshit

Larry D. Thomas

It luxuriates
in the thoughts of priests
who hide it under vestments

and mute its cacophony
in the fervor of solemn vows.
What is philosophy but tons of it

shoveled behind the barn of argument,
camouflaged with dazzle
in the ravishing prism of the syllogism?

For thousands of years it has swirled
in the brandy-snifter-ears of paramours
and been burped into utterances of devotion.

Only the cowhand has faced it for what it is
and turned its brooking into a career,
solely for the promise of a good steak.

Ain't Misbehavin'

Jeffrey Thomson

(*Nixon and Armstrong, 1952*)

In the buzzy neon and fresh vinyl of LAX,
two men come together, the senator from California

and a trumpet player, they come together around
the spinning black track the baggage claim

makes and grip each other's hand and
for a moment look like a photo and its negative.

I'm a big fan, says Nixon, smiling rich
as cream, *if there's ever anything I can do for you,*

just let me know. And to the surprise of everyone,
Armstrong shuffles his eyes down, says,

Well, suh, I got an extra bag an' if you could grab it
I'd be grateful. And everyone's watching now and now

Nixon's grin falls a little
but he's a little too good at his job

to be rattled and snatches the bag and carries it
through customs while the merry snickers

of the band follow him the way a wake follows a boat
into the dock. A blue marl of sky clouds the glasses

of the men who stand sentry around the senator
as the two men move toward the black silk

of their limos and Armstrong opens up
his picket-fence smile and accepts the bag back

with a shuck and a nod to the other layers
of the story, race riots and war, the thicket

of heat rising up the manzanita hills, lies ready to brushfire
their way through the American experience. And given

all he was and all that will happen—black-capped
burglars with their satchels, wiretaps hissing on the line—

I'm only too happy to show you Nixon humiliated here,
but who's to say that's the story; the future's still

blank as the glasses of the senator's men.
A circus of hands gathers the bags and stacks them

in the trunks of cars as the sunlight sloughs off
the twin aircraft parked nose to nose in the blooming heat.

Nixon knew what it meant to make a man a fool, but
Armstrong knew customs would never

search the senator and find the quarter pound
of Jamaican Pearl he'd hidden in that bag.

What Are You Reading?
Jeffrey Thomson

Let's pretend I am
reading your book,
and I enjoy it immensely.
It's your range that attracts
me: you put a mirror between
two mirrors and imagine
the infinite and its opposite.
You lecture the bees
in the furious work
of their hive. You bell
the cat and mouse
down into the hole
in the wall, white as
a blank page. The way
you take risks, too,
like a wing walker hung
from the stanchions
of a single engine Bellanca,
buffeted by the wind of all
those open vowels, the electric
froth of the clouds now
above you now below
and the plane dizzy
with your pyrotechnics,
I particularly admire. It's
all about danger, for you,
isn't it? The way you
stalk your poem through
the sea grass, filled like the sea
with all the plastic bangles
and coconuts jetsam can
manage, the long V
of the grass closing on
the heels of your poem
as it slips back toward
the trees and the small
house in the clearing
where you can still hear
the surf roughing up the
shore, and you, you predator
on after it. Now you
build beautiful contraptions
that snap shut around me,
now you let me free to
wander the trumpeting

fields of your imagination,
black-faced lambs nuzzling
clover while you, like the
kindest of shepherds, start
the slaughter—your knife
the color of moonlight—so as
to lay out lunch for the wolf.

Coming Clean at 13

David Vancil

I baptized myself late one night
while taking a hot bath, calling on
the Son, the Father, and Holy Ghost
to make me perfect. How satisfyingly I
answered mother's query if I was clean,
"Don't worry, Mother, I'll be out squeaky."
Yet I did other things in that tub anon
I'd rather not make a claim on. My quest
for goodness was replaced with longing,
as I sunk into seductive depths of bubbles,
steam, and suds that clung wetly like sin
to my pink skin. When dear Mother called
me then, I answered pithily: "I'm coming."
I never lied, albeit somehow I felt dirty.

In Tears

David Vancil

In Mexico, I made a pretty little girl cry
in a restaurant when I mixed genders,
transforming her with bad Spanish from a girl
to a boy. I recall she stewed over her pancakes,
pointing at me with a knife while complaining
to her mother of my *niño*. Why I laughed
I can't say, except she was cute. But then
her *madre* scowled at me then when I giggled.
In my homeland, I've made many women
miserable from my fecklessness, after I slipped
away, leaving not even a note behind. Why,
I'm unsure of, except I thought it their fault
that they flirted. No doubt I've offended men as well.
But let's not dwell on them. They deserved it.
Imagine me instead alone in a dark room
with no window, my face turned to the wall,
friendless. Feel sad for me. I know I will.

The Gospel according to Jeremy (The Second Cousin of Jesus [once removed], The Patron Saint of Drunk Artists

David Joez Villaverde

1. Carve out eyes
2. Visit apothecary
3. Recover. The sun is shining somewhere, this being both life affirming and an annoyance
4. Brush teeth for smile you'll never show
5. Stoop without stupor, in remembrance and offering
6. Saunter with imagined confidence, stagger under scrutiny
7. Fill in lacunae
8.
9. Ignore the cries of the great horned one. Sally forth with sexual impunity
10. Bow to the God of your mother's imagination, in deference and diffidence.
11. Forget the happy puppet who laughed in his cage. That is no longer you.
12. Struggle.
13. Always be distrustful of those whose services you depend on.
14. Be skeptical of those who abhor politics.
15. Beware of the apostates and heretics who conspicuously take up purpose
16. Blackout, when needed, to relieve yourself of the pains of being human
17. Carry with you a heap of regrets, to inform your heart
18. Swoon with whiskey, float with smoke
19. Look to the sky for answers, do not expect any
20. Judge those who would allow it
21. Turn off ears, brain
22. Fill glass, lift, repeat
23. Never forget what drives men to create ornate hoaxes
24. Live as a reminder of intent
25. Disdain fluoridation, and water in general
26. Care for others with all of your being, but express this poorly
27. Visit apothecary again
28. Favor music over somnolence.
29. Name you children after saints, eschew other traditions that bore you
30. Don't associate with Welshmen, Scots or Britons. Ever.
31. Drink as if tomorrow you might not be able to
32. ~~Destroy everything you value~~
32. Destroy everything of value
33. Remember to humor those that speak of interstitial strategies. Only scavengers and vermin relegate themselves to the liminal places
34. Excrete art on the road to death.
35. Repeat. Fill glass, lift, repeat.

The Art of Laziness
Jason Walker

A needle crashed
into the cement
like the fish
the delivery boy tossed
into yards
instead of papers.
God canned him.

A mutt glorifies the ground:
his leg raised up,
praise falling down.
A pigeon struts
to the snow cone,
stutters his head as if saying,
"It's not as filling as the bread
sacrificed from those virgin mamas,
but I take what He gives."

A man fish-hooks
and reels a woman's whale purse
into his shopping ship.
He puts it on
top of coins and creased dollars
that line the bottom
of his drifting bucket.

Jesus bites his other cheek
and swims through the crowd.

My beard is bigger than his.

On the Road to Music City

Jason Walker

"Jackson Pollock's *Number 8* blows compared to
your floorboard." My brother
La-Z-Boys
the passenger
seat, denting the empty
box behind him. I sock the gas with my bare foot

before the light gleams red. An hour later, his snores
are as humdrum as the
country pop
tunes fumbling
on the radio. "I'll
staple your mouth shut." But his cauliflower dreams

are too steamy. He won't wake up till Nashville. Rain
whips the windshield. Blue
lights? I swear
all cops are—
"Sir, your left headlight is
out"—heroic. My brother readjusts the seat

to a ninety-degree angle, swabbing his ear
with his pinky. "Offer
that boar some
barbeque
next time," he says with parched
eyes. In the rain, we duct tape a flashlight to the grill.

On the Romantic/Anti-Social Side of the Beach Where the Sunsets Are the Most Inspirational/Depressing

Jason Walker

"I make weal and create woe"—Isaiah 45:7

Once they're gone, I wipe out *Jimmy*
Loves Leslie with my heel

because *Fuck You* Jimmy and Leslie.
The tide's pulled lower than their swimsuits,
and the sand's soggier than my pits. Dead jellyfish
shrivel up, their tentacles strings of phlegm.

The phone I spent my whole paycheck on
dips in a wave.
whine
4 weeks ago: *All you do is whine whine.* (She dumptrucked

a bucket of pecans onto my head.) *Don't be mad.*
(Then I humped my way up the tree that birthed
the pecans . . .) *Come back, you vag.* (. . . till I dropped
like a nut.) *I needed giant mitts to catch you.*

In the sea, the fish will bus along
until they wreck into a net, and after,
when cleaved, I'll devour them
as if they're me. I shake my shoes

at the stars; they think they're so
pretty, and—damn it—they are.

Bluto's Plea to Olive Oyl
Will Wells

You really need to dump the jerk—
that psycho who stuffs spinach in his pipe.
Talk about dangers of second-hand smoke!
The moron brags about "MUSKULS."
His largest squats between his ears,
his smallest one between his legs.
He sucks down cans of leafy Red Bull
like a human sinkhole.
But that doesn't explain his mood swings,
sudden rages, shrunken testes
and those male breasts he flexes
up and down like pistons while steam
blares factory whistles from his ears.
It's only a matter of time
till he buys an assault rifle
and wipes out Gold's Gym.

And you, my shiny one, sizzling
in the pan of my imagination,
my recipe for a healthy heart,
your one spit curl like the hand of God
extended in the Sistine Chapel.
You are the real eye-popper!
Come live with me, and be my condiment, O!
And I will be your red pimento.

Sestina
Tom Whalen

The sestina is a form that has six
stanzas and an envoi. The words
at the end of each line permute
mathematically. Sometimes it pisses
me off when I can't make sense
of the form, but usually it's easy.

The sestina is a form that's easy.
It has an envoi and stanzas six.
At the end of each line is sense.
Mathematically I think the words,
whether or not I can make piss
of this form, usually permute.

So the sestina is a form that permutes.
Its stanzas and envoi are easy.
At the end of each line I piss
mathematically. Sometimes it's six
me's jerking off when I can't find words
for this form, but usually it makes sense.

The sestina is a form prone to nonsense.
Its stanzas and envoi permute.
At the end of each line is a word.
Mathematically I find all this easy.
Me, you, me, you, me, you, six
jerkoffs in search of a form to piss

in, that's the sestina form, a French piss-
er standing over a trough of nonsense
like a milk cow in a barn, no, six
cows and a mathematical dwarf permuted
into me and you trying to ease
our way into (out of) this barn of words.

The sestina is a form that has words.
Its stanzas and envoi piss.
At the end of each line it's easy
to, mathematically, make sense.
Me, I think I've permuted
this form so much, that six

seems the only word that makes sense.
Six, six, six, six, six, six, it's easy.
Go permute. I'd rather piss.

The Best of Intentions
Harold Whit Williams

I've always wanted to teach Garrison Keillor
How to play guitar. I'm sure he already owns
An antique Gibson, or a prewar Martin,
Signed at Gruhn's in Nashville by some
Graying country and western legend. I'm sure

He can already fumble his way through
"Love Me Tender," or "Hey, Good Lookin',"
But I want this fellow to really shred!
Plug him in to a Marshall stack, squeeze
Him into those miniscule Angus Young

Schoolboy shorts, then watch him prance
Amidst the dry ice fog, the laser lights.
I've always taken things too far. I dreamt
This poem, then wrote it down.
I've said too much already.

Emergency Exit Procedures

Harold Whit Williams

If I could have your attention
For just one moment please.
I am the bearded gentleman
Next to you in coach, quietly
Drowning in scotch and sodas.
I sell mattresses in St. Louis.
I am poet laureate of seat 26D.
Please return your serving tray
To its upright position. As you
Can imagine, each puffy cloud
We spy at thirty thousand feet
Was once someone's bedtime wish
Or prayer. This way of thinking
Surely pleases those dreary deities
We dreamt up. The very ones
Working on super-storms, or
Stronger strains of an influenza.
I design smartbombs in Virginia.
I panhandle for peace at the base
Of Mt. Rushmore. Please remain
Seated with your seatbelt fastened.
Each feral horse galloping the grass-
Lands beneath us is a stray thought
In meditation. Each bleached bone
In the drought-dry gulch shines
Like some sharp incisor of Satan.
My youth minister spoke of demons.
He could see them leeched on to
A sinner's back, and always said—
If your heart is a house, unlock
The front door for Jesus! Unlatch
Windows! Leave the balcony open!
He never performed his exorcism
On me, and these days I do itch
Madly between my shoulder blades.
But I've grown accustomed to
That extra weight back there. It
Keeps me steady on ground, in air.
Keeps me from falling face forward
Into the cold hard kingdom of heaven.

How To Talk to Kids About Death
Harold Whit Williams

Appear at midnight, out of nowhere
Like some snippet from a dream,
But leave your wig and clown nose
Back at the office. Chuckle softly,

Toot your silly little horn. Start
With interpretive dance, then
Throw in Tuvan throat singing. Sit
Cross-legged at the foot of the bed,

Beatnik-snapping your fingers.
Warm their tiny, sticky hands
In your big fat bear paws, gently
Squeezing to accentuate words

Like *love* and *loss* and *defibrillator*.
Finish with a flourish of French
Surrealist couplets, and by no means
Answer any questions that arise.

The Known Unknowns
Harold Whit Williams

"I thought he might slip me the answer."
—John Lennon, explaining his helicopter ride with the Maharishi

At the exact same moment astronomers
Discover another universe, not parallel
But damn near the same as ours, my
Large thin-crust four cheese extra
Garlic with side salads becomes
One minute late—two times.
Free delivery, it says right here
And also, way over there. We inhabit,
Of course, this slightly crooked
Carbon-based copy. All of our
Ice Capades, beauty pageants, boy
Bands and suicide bombers, atrocity
Facsimiles light years away from
The originals. Seems it lets us all
Off the hook. My hand wringing,
Your shower singing of show tunes.
Our lost elections, championship
Games, virginities. And I cannot
Stand it when they don't slice all
The way through the pie, then forget
Those little parmesan packets. Also,
How hard news keeps happening,
How weather keeps changing, how
Time talks hush-toned sense to me
Like some hangdog sober friend
At the New Year's Eve party.
Or to misquote Robert Pinsky—
When I have nothing, it will
Not be a moment too soon.

El Poema
Robert E. Wood

When you are not looking at it
this poem is in Spanish
and it rhymes beautifully

When this poem is in Spanish
it means something entirely different
and it inspires and delights everyone

After you finish reading this poem
it will, once again, be in Spanish
Comme blague, le dernier vers est français

"Buzzard Starts Fire": Texas Newspaper Headline
R. Scott Yarbrough

I imagine him some delinquent adolescent buzzard,
misunderstood, with some arsenal of box matches
on a mission, wearing a placard, "Buzzards
are people, too," flying his mission: lofty,
prideful, strong, vengeful, determined to set
a fire at any suicidal cost, to burn Texas
down to its cowboy boots and rusty spurs.

The summer has been hot here in Dallas,
record heat, the soil is cracked the size
of black Texas Ranger baseball bats: drought. The sad
scientific reality is that the black bird of the animal
kingdom – not by choice, but by genetic code –
simply crawled up the hot sky to try to sit
in the slight breeze, his dehydrated body balanced
on a wire like a dizzied trapeze artist losing
his momentary balance, his talon lifting
slightly, enough for the current to jump
the synaptic gap like touching
the grey steel band around the hole
in the heart of the cartoon man
in the kid's game Operation.

His nose lights up red, an alarm buzzes.
He spontaneously combusts, a ball of fire
falling, flapping. We've all burned
our hair once – that smell. His blazing
body licked the dead grass alive in flame.
Buzzard starts fire.
The irony is his too burned
body is not even palatable enough
to be eaten by his own mirrored kind.

This Little Piggy
R. Scott Yarbrough

Mother left we three boys in the finned Fairlane,
West Texas windows rolled down, a quick zip into
the Piggly Wiggly for whole milk and Log Cabin syrup.

My oldest brother, Don, noticed the green face of the
dollar bill first on the asphalt waving its corner
like a gift. The middle brother, Steve, came

up with the idea that if each one held one
leg, then they could lower me to retrieve
the prize. They dropped me on my head.

I got the dollar and stood crying by
the door of the car. Don talked Horace Crenshaw
into putting me back through the window

for fifty cents: Horace drank cough medicine
and aftershave; he took the dollar and gave
us back two quarters. Steve said he and

Don would clean the blood off my forehead
for a quarter each so mother wouldn't spank me
when she got back for being bloody for no reason.

All the way home I see myself as a little
cartoon Piggly Wiggly pig wearing
a diaper, my voice stuffed shut with that proverbial

red apple, a sort of Adam infant dropped
on asphalt left to noun my new terrain.
This little pig knew then, I was all on my own.

Ransom

Kevin Zepper

. . . now listen closely and listen good. I have your poem and if you don't do what you're told, you won't see your poem again—ever! I'm not going to hang on this cell long so don't pull anything tricky. Sounds like you got the little present I sent you. Yeah, I cut a line off your precious poem to prove I mean business. Yeah, yeah, call me what you want but I've got your little verse tucked away and I'm calling the shots. Here are my demands: I want a complete, unabridged set of the Oxford English Dictionary, the index, too. No condensed version crap either. The real deal. Meet me behind the Noble Barn at midnight. Go to the second dumpster where they ditch the tear covers and romance returns. Stuff the OED in a big black lawn bag, two-ply, and put it on top of the dumpster lid. I'll set the poem in its place after I know no one's followed me. Let me be clear on this, if you drag the English Department in, I'll have to cut your poem a little more and a little more . . . . Be a smart poet and don't try anything heroic. I have a degree in American Lit and I'm not afraid to use it . . . .

Second Chance
Kevin Zepper

Do you remember
that one time
when we tried
to pick up chicks
at the Second Chance Thrift Store?

It was a Friday afternoon,
nothing to do,
'cept smoke cigs,
and chug soda
right outta the bottle,
sitting on the curb,
scoping things out.

We walked in,
The bell jingled above us,
not one of the dozen odd
thrift chicks even looked.

It was a red tag sale,
stuff an old grocery bag
full of stuff
for a buck.

We were tagless guys,
from the bottom shelf,
and totally green.

Post Office Tryst
Bob Ziller

An Emily Dickinson stamp,
amazing—
it moans when you lick it!

Weather Girls
Richard Lee Zuras

January late and the leotard dressed weather
girl on that southern cable station giggles
"Imagine that much snow falling."

She is looking off screen
at her green screen. Arms flail up and down
through I-95 corridor, a manicured nail stops,

arrows Manhattan, Philadelphia drifts up
toward Boston. My wife and I do not find
weather girl amusing. In any way. We sip

beers and gun insults. Like Elvis.

       .

These weather girls who lunch in Savannah
chortle: "I've never even *seen* measurable snow . . ."
as Al Roker laments NYC
where snow was close to 70 inches
for the winter.

My wife and I
here in Maine
still can't open our front door

the drifts too high

         (and back to Al in NYC)

"This was a harsh winter," he says
standing on dry pavement in April.
My wife fires her Schlitz at his face

(Elvis style). I fist back the curtain
stand tippy-toe and peer over the drift.
"It's snowing," I say. My wife squats

next to the RCA and points to where
the crown of Maine would be

if leotard girl would get out of the way. We're
here she says. Then she whispers
we're here.

Contributors

Michael Albright has published poems in various journals, including *Stirring, Rust + Moth, Tar River Poetry, Pembroke Magazine, Cider Press Review, Pretty Owl, Uppagus*, and has a forthcoming chapbook, *In the Hall of Dead Birds and Viking Tools* (Finishing Line, 2015). He lives near Greensburg, Pennsylvania, with his wife, Lori.

Dorothy Alexander, author of 4 poetry collections and a memoir, is a founding member of the Oklahoma Woody Guthrie Poets and curates a monthly poetry reading in Oklahoma City. She embraces a form she calls "narcissistic narrative," and she often indulges in "selfie" poetry.

Brian Allgar, although immutably English, lives in Paris. He started entering humorous competitions in 1967, but took a 35-year break, re-emerging in 2011 as a kind of Rip Van Winkle of the competition world. He drinks malt whisky and writes music, which may explain his fondness for Mendelssohn's "Scottish" Symphony.

Fred Alsberg received his MFA from the University of Arkansas in Fayetteville. He has published poems in *Greensboro Review, Louisiana Review*, the *Southeast Review, Rhino*, and *Oklahoma Today*.

Lloyd Aquino teaches composition, literature, and creative writing at Mount San Antonio College. He has no idea what is so goddamn funny.

Barbara Astor lives in Bellbrook, Ohio. Her poetry has appeared in *Concho River Review, Avocet, Kaleidoscope, Lilliput Review, The Lyric, Tiger's Eye*, and *Brevities*. She is the author of two poetry collections, *Thirty Years Past* (2011) and *High into the Blue* (2013), published by Finishing Line Press.

Barbara Astor lives in Bellbrook, Ohio.Her poetry, in part, has appeared in *Concho River Review, Avocet, Kaleidoscope, Lilliput Review, The Lyric, Tiger's Eye*, and *Brevities*. She is the author of 2 poetry collections published by Finishing Line Press including *Thirty Years Past* (2011) and *High Into the Blue* (2013).

Michael Baldwin, a self-professed descendent of Lakota mystic warrior Crazy Horse, was born and reared in Fort Worth, Texas, amid the olfactory cornucopia of its stock yards, rendering plants, and chemical factories. He was a library administrator and professor of American government until he wasn't. Mike resides in Benbrook, Texas.

Melissa Balmain is the Editor of *Light*, America's premier journal of light verse. Her poetry collection *Walking In on People* (winner of the Able Muse Book Award) is often assumed by online shoppers to be some kind of porn.

Carolyn Banks is a novelist, journalist, and essayist who lives in Bastrop, Texas. She teaches at Austin Community College. She writes a weekly humor column called "Piece of Mind" for the *Bastrop Advertiser* and the *Austin American-Statesman* website. Her 1980s thriller, *The Darkroom*, was recently republished by Author's Guild.

Walter Bargen has published 18 books of poetry. His most recent books are *Days Like This Are Necessary: New & Selected Poems* (2009), *Endearing Ruins* (2012), *Trouble behind Glass Doors* (2013), *Quixotic* (2014), and *Gone West* (2014). He was appointed the first poet laureate of Missouri (2008-2009). See www.walterbargen.com.

Tony Barnstone is a poet, critic, translator, and anthologist and the author of 18 books including 5 books of poetry, most recently Pulp Sonnets (Tupelo Press 2015) and Beast in the Apartment (Sheep Meadow Press 2014). He teaches at Whittier College.

Joan E. Bauer is the author of *The Almost Sound of Drowning* (Main Street Rag, 2008). Her poems have appeared or are forthcoming in *Chiron Review, Confrontation, The Paterson Literary Review, Slipstream*, and

US 1 Worksheets. With Jimmy Cvetic, she co-hosts and curates the Hemingway's Summer Poetry Series, www.hemingwayspoetryseries.blogspot.com.

Trudi C. Beckman writes, "The poem was written after a long afternoon of cleaning a department's refrigerator; fittingly, a decomposition of Coleridge's 'Rhyme of the Ancient Mariner.' I have moved on to another department, where I no longer clean refrigerators, but luxuriate in processing paperwork and drinking coffee."

Kate Bernadette Benedict of Riverdale, New York, is the non-heroic author of *Earthly Use: New and Selected Poems*, published in 2015. Previous collections are *Here from Away* and *In Company*. Kate edited the erstwhile poetry journals *Umbrella* and *Tilt-a-Whirl*; archives are online and linked from her home page at www.katebenedict.com.

Alan Berecka earns his keep as reference librarian at Del Mar College in Corpus Christi. His poetry has appeared in *American Literary Review, The Christian Century, The Texas Review,* and the anthology *St Peter's B-List* (Ava Maria Press). His latest poetry collection is *With Our Baggage* (Lamar University Press, 2013).

Jane Blanchard lives and writes in Georgia. Her poetry has recently appeared in *The Evansville Review, The Rotary Dial, Thema,* and *US 1 Worksheets.* Her chapbook, *Unloosed,* is forthcoming from White Violet Press.

CL Bledsoe's latest collection is *Riceland.* His latest novel is *Man of Clay.* He currently lives in northern Virginia with his daughter.

Daniel Bosch's poems, translations, essays, and reviews are legible at online journals such as *Slate, Agni, B O D Y, 3 A.M. Magazine, The Daily Beast, The Fortnightly Review,* and *Berfrois,* where he is senior editor. He teaches writing at Emory University.

James Bowden writes that nothing is interesting about him, and he is not at all academic. In retirement he divides his time amongst pipe smoking, grandfathering, some writing, and a bit of painting. He is the Odd Job of the family. "Ten grandchildren! I am pleased with that last bit."

Matthew Brennan has published 4 volumes of poetry and 2 chapbooks. His next collection, *One Life,* is forthcoming from Lamar University Literary Press. His most recent book, *The House with the Mansard Roof* (2009), was a finalist for the Best Books of Indiana. He teaches at Indiana State University.

Cory Brown is the author of 4 books of poems. His poems have appeared in *Bomb, Nimrod International,* and *Postmodern Culture,* among other journals. His essays have appeared in *The International Journal of Technology, Knowledge, Society and Diner,* and in the most recent issue of *South Loop Review.*

Nathan Brown, Poet Laureate of Oklahoma for 2013-2014, is a songwriter and award-winning poet from Wimberley, Texas. Of his 11 books, *Karma Crisis: New and Selected Poems* was a finalist for the 2013 Paterson Poetry Prize and the Oklahoma Book Award. *Two Tables Over* won the 2009 Oklahoma Book Award.

Denise C. Buschmann is a freelance writer, editor, and proofreader. A former teacher, she holds master's degrees in mild interventions and reading from The University of Indianapolis. She organized and coordinates the Indiana chapter of Editorial Freelancers Association (EFA) and has been published in numerous journals at home and abroad.

Don Kingfisher Campbell has been a poetryholic for 38 years. He supports his habit by hosting a reading/workshop series at the Santa Catalina Branch of the Pasadena Public Library. He even got one of those MFA thingys recently at Antioch University. For tales of his public exposures go to http://dkc1031.blogspot.com.

Michael Cantor's full-length collection, *Life in the Second Circle* (Able Muse Press, 2012), was a finalist for the 2013 Massachusetts Book Award for Poetry. A chapbook, *The Performer*, was published in 2007. His work has appeared in all the usual suspects.

Alan Catlin worked for 34 years in the bar business honing verbal skills germane to projects such as this one. He has been writing a long series under the working title of "Alien Nation," which he considers social commentary disguised as bar poems. His current work in progress is called "Hollyweird."

Catherine Chandler is the author of *Lines of Flight*, shortlisted for the Poets' Prize, *Glad and Sorry Seasons*, and *This Sweet Order*. She is the winner of the Howard Nemerov Sonnet Award, the Leslie Mellichamp Prize, and *The Lyric* Quarterly Prize. Welcome aboard her poetry blog, "The Wonderful Boat" (www.cathychandler.blogspot.com)!

Robert Cooperman, lifelong Deadhead, is the author of numerous poetry collections, some less scatological than others. *Just Drive* (Brick Road Poetry Press) is about Cooperman's cab driving in NYC in the mid-1970s. *The Words We Used* (Main Street Rag) describes growing up on the less than mean streets of Brooklyn.

Sarah Cortez, Councilor of the Texas Institute of Letters, won the PEN Texas Literary Award in Poetry. Her book *Cold Blue Steel* was a finalist in the Writers' League of Texas awards. She's won a Southwest Book Award and several ILBAs. She's been finalist for both Texas and Houston Poet Laureate.

Sherry Craven's writing appears in numerous anthologies including *Goodbye Mexico*, *Her Texas*, *descant*, and *The Texas Review*. She has poetry coming out in *Stone Renga*, *RiverSedge*, *Southern Poetry Anthology*, *VIII: Texas*. She won the Conference of College Teachers of English Poetry Award. Her book is entitled *Standing at the Window*. www.sherrycraven.com

Dallas Crow teaches English at Breck School in Golden Valley, Minnesota. He is the author of a chapbook, *Small, Imperfect Paradise* (Parallel Press).

Chip Dameron is the author of a travel book and 7 collections of poetry including *Waiting for an Etcher* (Lamar University Press 2015) and *Drinking from the River: New and Selected Poems, 1975-2015* (Wings Press). A member of the Texas Institute of Letters, he lives in Brownsville, Texas.

William Virgil Davis has published 6 books of poetry, most recently *Dismantlements of Silence: Poems Selected and New* (2015). His other books are *The Bones Poems*; *Landscape and Journey*; *Winter Light*; *The Dark Hours*; *One Way To Reconstruct the Scene*, which won the Yale Series of Younger Poets Prize.

Paul Dickey has published 2 full-length collections of poems, *Wires Over the Homeplace* (Pinyon Publishing, 2013) and *They Say This Is How Death Came into the World* (Mayapple Press, 2011). His work appears in over 100 literary journals including frequent appearances in *Concho River Review*. His personal website is http://pauldickey9.wix.com/paul-dickey.

Colin Dodds is an author, poet, and screenwriter. His writing has appeared in more than 200 publications, been nominated and shortlisted for numerous prizes, and has been praised by luminaries including Norman Mailer and David Berman. He lives in Brooklyn, New York, with his wife, Samantha. See his work at thecolindodds.com.

Tom Dodge is an old dog, living in Midlothian, Texas, and uninterested in learning new tricks. His dream of learning the post-modern trick failed when he barked the notes of "The Star Spangled Banner" backwards and the audience stoned him. Now he no longer even shakes hands or begs for food.

George Drew is author of *The View from Jackass Hill* (X. J. Kennedy Poetry Prize, Texas Review Press, 2011.) *Fancy's Orphan* is due out in 2017 (Tiger Bark Press), and *Pastoral Habits* (Texas Review Press) in 2016. *Down & Dirty*, a chapbook, was released in 2015 from Texas Review Press.

Millard Dunn's books include *Shakespeare's Sonnets: This Powerful Rhyme* (with Ken Watson, Phoenix Education: Sidney, Australia, 2005), *Engraved on Air* (The Kentucky Arts Council, 1983), and *Places We Could Never Find Alone* (Ink Brush Press, 2011).

Maureen DuRant lives in Medicine Park, Oklahoma, and teaches at Cameron University. Her work has appeared or is forthcoming in *Crosstimbers*, *Red River Review*, and *Westview* and is featured on the refrigerator doors of several relatives. She is currently a student in the Queens University of Charlotte Low Residency MFA program.

Andrea Eames is a Zimbabwean writer living in Austin, Texas, after 8 years in New Zealand. She has released 2 novels, *The Cry of the Go-Away Bird* and *The White Shadow*, both published by Random House.

Meg Eden's work has been published in *Rattle*, *Drunken Boat*, *Poet Lore*, and *Gargoyle*. She teaches at the University of Maryland. She has published 4 chapbooks, and her novel, *Post-High School Reality Quest*, is forthcoming from California Coldblood, an imprint of Rare Bird Lit. Check out her work at www.megedenbooks.com.

Chris Ellery is the author of 3 poetry collections, most recently *The Big Mosque of Mercy*, poems of the Middle East. He is co-translator of *Whatever Happened to Antara* by award-winning Syrian writer Walid Ikhlassi. A member of the Texas Institute of Letters, Ellery currently teaches at Angelo State University.

Joe Garland is a student at Angelo State University. He enjoys drawing, meditating, and reading. His biggest influences are Peyo, Kipling, and P.G. Wodehouse.

Author of *Humor Me* (David Robert Books, 2006), finalist for the Nemerov Sonnet Award, and semifinalist for the Anthony Hecht Poetry Prize, Claudia Gary writes, edits, sings, and composes (tonally) near Washington, DC. Her articles on health appear in *The VVA Veteran*, *VFW*, and elsewhere. See http://www.pw.org/content/claudia_gary.

Mark Goad is a poet living on Cape Cod, Massachusetts. Educated in English and German literature, theology, and philosophy, he has been published in *Assisi*, *Corvus*, *Decanto*, *Turbulence*, *Big River Literary Review*, *Extracts*, *Crannóg*, *Ayris*, *The Wayfarer*, *Boston Poetry Magazine*, *Contrary*, *Turbulence*, *Christian Century*, *Poetry Salzburg Review*, and *Spiritus*.

Lyman Grant is a professor of creative writing and humanities at Austin Community College (Texas). He is the editor of the *Letters of Roy Bedichek* and *New Growth: Contemporary Short Stories by Texas Writers*. He has published 3 volumes of poetry and one chapbook.

Jonathan Greenhause was a finalist or received honorable mention in recent poetry contests from *Naugatuck River Review*, *New Millennium Writings*, *Peregrine*, *Red Hen Press*, and *River Styx*. He has poems in or forthcoming from *The Bitter Oleander*, *The Dark Horse*, *Fjords*, *New Walk Magazine*, *Quarter after Eight*, *RHINO*, and *Stand*.

Maryanne Hannan has published recent poetry in *Rattle*, *Gargoyle*, *Light Quarterly*, *WomenArts Quarterly*, *Windhover*, and *Minnesota Review*. A former Latin teacher, she lives in upstate New York. Her website is www.mhannan.com.

Michelle Hartman's work, featured in *Langdon Review of the Arts in Texas*, appears in over 60 journals in America and overseas and over 30 anthologies. Her poetry books, *Irony and Irreverence* and *Disenchanted and Disgruntled* (Lamar University Press), are available on Amazon. She is the editor of *Red River Review*.

Johnny Hartner is a native of Pittsburgh, a CCAC professor with degrees from Carnegie Mellon and Duquesne University. He is eternally grateful to his mentor, Elias Abdou, for all he's learned in teaching, writing, and publishing.

Michael Harty divides time and energies between his writing and day job as psychologist and psychoanalyst in Prairie Village, Kansas, which is neither a village nor on the prairie but a suburb of Kansas City. Poems appear or are forthcoming in *Midwest Quarterly*, *The Lyric*, *New Letters*, and *Kansas City Voices*.

Happily freed from faculty meetings and term papers, Jan D. Hodge spends his time writing double-dactyl narratives, various poetry challenges, and occasionally a serious poem or two. *Taking Shape*, his collection of *carmina figurata*, was recently published by Able Muse Press.

Katherine Hoerth is the author of 2 poetry collections, *Goddess Wears Cowboy Boots* (Lamar University Press, 2014), which received the Helen C. Smith Prize from the Texas Institute of Letters, and *The Garden Uprooted* (Slough Press, 2012). Katherine teaches English at the University of Texas Rio Grande Valley.

Lynn Hoffman was born in Brooklyn and lives in Philadelphia. Among his published books are *Radiation Days*, a comedy about cancer, and *Short Course in Beer*, a very serious but tasty book about ales and lagers.

Originally from the United States, Sally Houtman has made her home in Wellington, New Zealand, since 2005. She has been known to string occasional words together to form sentences and paragraphs which inadvertently come together as poems and stories. Once, completely by accident, she wrote an entire book.

Ann Howells has edited *Illya's Honey* since 1999, recently going digital at www.IllyasHoney.com. Her chapbooks are *Black Crow in Flight* (Main Street Rag, 2007) and *The Rosebud Diaries* (Willet, 2012). Her book *Under a Lone Star*, illustrated by artist Darrell Kirkley, is forthcoming from Village Books Press early in 2016.

Andrew Hudgins is the author, most recently, of *The Joker: A Memoir* (Simon Schuster, 2013) and *A Clown at Midnight* (Houghton Mifflin Harcourt, 2013). He is Humanities Distinguished Professor in English at The Ohio State University.

Marc Jampole wrote *Music from Words*, published by Bellday Books (2007). His poetry has appeared in *Evansville Review*, *Mississippi Review*, *Cortland Review*, *Vallum*, *Slant*, *Cutthroat*, *Ellipsis*, and other journals. More than 1,500 of his freelance articles have been published in magazines and newspapers. Marc also writes the popular OpEdge blog.

A PhD student in humanities with a creative writing focus at University of Texas Dallas, Mark Allen Jenkins is former editor-in-chief for *Reunion: The Dallas Review*. His poems have appeared in *Memorious, Minnesota Review, South Dakota Review*, and *Every River on Earth: Writing from Appalachian Ohio*, and is forthcoming in *Gargoyle*.

Hank Jones "teaches" at Tarleton State University. He suspects the grading of freshman papers has made him stupider. Having given up poetry as a youthful indiscretion, he has recently started writing again because why not. His poetry has appeared in *Cybersoleil, Voices de la Luna*, and *Dragon Poet Review*.

Steven G. Kellman is a professor of comparative literature at the University of Texas at San Antonio. His books include *Redemption: The Life of Henry Roth, The Translingual Imagination*, and *The Self-Begetting Novel*. He is a recipient of the National Book Critics Circle's Nona Balakian Citation for Excellence in Reviewing.

Jennifer Kidney is a freelance scholar and adjunct assistant professor for the College of Liberal Studies at the University of Oklahoma. She is the author of 6 books of poetry; her most recent collection, *Road Work Ahead*, was published by Village Books Press in 2012.

Cindy King's work has appeared in *Callaloo, North American Review, African American Review, Cimarron Review, Black Warrior Review, American Literary Review, Jubilat*, and elsewhere. She received a Tennessee Williams Scholarship from the Sewanee Writers' Conference and the Agha Shahid Ali Prize. She teaches at the University of North Texas Dallas.

James Henry Knippen teaches at Texas State University. His poems have appeared in *Colorado Review, Mid-American Review, The Missouri Review Online, 32 Poems, Hayden's Ferry Review, Denver Quarterly, Blackbird*, and *West Branch*, among other journals.

Joe R. Lansdale is the author of over 40 novels and numerous short stories. His work has received many awards and stories. *Bubba Hotep* and *Cold in July* have been filmed. Next year Sundance Channel will debut *Hap and Leonard* based on his crime series.

John B. Lee is Poet Laureate of the city of Brantford and Norfolk County. The most recent of his 75 published books is *The Full Measure* (Black Moss Press, 2015) and *The Secret Second Language of the Heart* (Sanbun Publishing, 2015). He lives in Port Dover, Ontario, Canada.

Wayne Lee was born in British Columbia and raised in Bellingham, Washington. He is married to poet/painter Alice Lee and lives in Hillsboro, Oregon, where he works as an editor and educator. He won the 2012 Mark Fisher Poetry Prize, the 2012 SICA Poems for Peace Award, and the 2006 *Santa Fe Reporter* War Poetry Contest.

Michael Mark is a hospice volunteer and long distance walker. His poetry has appeared or is forthcoming in *Gargoyle Magazine, Lost Coast Review, Rattle, Ray's Road Review, Spillway, Tar River Poetry*, and *Sugar House Review*. His poetry has been nominated for the Pushcart Prize. Website: michaeljmark.com.

David Michael Martinez has been published in a variety of journals, most recently online at *Label Me Latina/o: The Journal of Twentieth and Twenty First Centuries Latino Literary Production*, and *Flies, Cockroaches, and Poets* (Fresno State MFA Journal).

Janet McCann is an old Texas poet who has been teaching at Texas A&M University since 1969, and this is her last semester. She was awarded an NEA grant in 1989. Her most recent book is *The Crone at the Casino* (Lamar University Press, 2014).

Jerry McElveen writes, "This dramatic monologue is based on the traditions brought over by Sicilian settlers to my hometown of Independence, Louisiana. It is NOT meant to be disrespectful of the Catholic Church or of my cherished Sicilian-American friends." His email address is jerrymackattack@yahoo.com.

Bryce Milligan, a folksinger/songwriter and a maker of guitars, drums and dulcimers, has been the publisher, editor, and designer for Wings Press since 1995.

John Graves Morris, Professor of English at Cameron University, is the author of *Noise and Stories* (Plain View Press, 2008). He is finishing a second collection entitled *Unwritten Histories*. His poems have appeared in *The Chariton Review*, *The Concho River Review*, *The Red Earth Review*, and *The Red River Review*.

karla k. morton, 2010 Texas Poet Laureate, is a Councilor of the Texas Institute of Letters and a Texas A&M graduate. Described as "one of the most adventurous voices in American poetry," she is a Betsy Colquitt Award Winner, twice an Indie National Book Award Winner, and has 10 poetry collections.

Tom Murphy has a chapbook titled *Horizon to Horizon* (2015) and poems in 2016 *Texas Poetry Calendar*, *Beatitude*, *Centrifuge*, *Nebula*, *Strike*, *Red River Review*, *Voices de la Luna*, *Switchgrass Review*, *Outrage: A Protest Anthology for Injustice in a Post 9/11 World* anthology, and the *Chupacabra* anthology.

Laurence Musgrove is a professor of English at Angelo State University where he teaches literature, creative writing, comics, and drawing-to-learn. His poems have appeared in *New Texas*, *Buddhist Poetry Review*, *Elephant Journal*, and *Concho River Review*. His poetry collection, *Local Bird*, was published by Lamar University Press in 2015.

Dave Newman is the author of 5 books including *The Poem Factory*, the novel *Two Small Birds*, and the collection *The Slaughterhouse Poems* (White Gorilla Press, 2013), named one of the best books of the year by *L Magazine*. He lives in Trafford with his wife, the writer Lori Jakiela.

Chris O'Carroll is a poet, actor, and stand-up comedian. So he has 3 ways of not making a living. He has been a featured poet in *Light* and has been anthologized in *Poems for a Liminal Age* (although he's right on the edge of not even knowing what "liminal" means).

Dave Parsons, 2011 Texas Poet Laureate, is recipient of a NEH Dante Fellowship to SUNY, the French/American Legation Poetry Prize, *Texas Review* Poetry Prize, and Baskerville Publisher's Prize and was inducted into The Texas Institute of Letters in 2009. He has published 6 poetry collections and teaches at LSC-Montgomery. See www.daveparsonspoetry.com.

Simon Perchik is an attorney whose poems have appeared in *Partisan Review*, *The Nation*, *Poetry*, *Osiris*, and *The New Yorker*. His collection *Almost Rain* was published by River Otter Press in 2013. For free e-books and his essay titled "Magic, Illusion and Other Realities," please visit his website at www.simonperchik.com.

George Perreault has published 3 collections of poetry, including *All the Verbs for Knowing* (Black Rock Press). He is currently completing a collection of narrative poems set on the Llanos Estacado.

Walt Peterson lives and teaches in Pittsburgh. He won the Acorn-Rukeyser award for poetry and is an artist on the Pennsylvania Council on the Arts and a Fellow of the Western Pennsylvania Writing Project.

Richard Pflum was born and continues to exist in Indianapolis. He lived in several other places after being drafted into the Army. He has a B.S. in chemistry although he wanted to be a classical musician. Lack of talent in music resulted in the uncovering of his literary aspirations.

Kenneth Pobo has books forthcoming from Blue Light Press (*Bend of Quiet*) and Urban Farmhouse Press (*Booking Rooms in the Kuiper Belt*). He teaches English and creative writing at Widener University in Pennsylvania.

Leslie Provence lives and writes in San Antonio. Despite being a wise ass, she has held on to her day job for 25 years and counting.

Mike Pulley is a journalist, poet, and senior lecturer in the Clemson University English department. His poems have appeared in *Cold Mountain Review, Canary, Café Review,* and *The South Carolina Review,* among others. In 2008 he was named a Pioneer Poet by the Sacramento Metropolitan Arts Commission.

Elizabeth Raby is the author of 4 poetry collections, the most recent of which is *Beneath Green Rain* (vacpoetry.org/purple-flag 2015), a memoir, *Ransomed Voices* (redmountainpress.us 2013), and 4 chapbooks. Winner of the 2010 Elmer Kelton Poetry Award, Angelo State University, she has been nominated several times for the Pushcart Prize.

Charles Rammelkamp edits *The Potomac,* an online literary journal, and is the prose editor for *BrickHouse Books* in Baltimore, Maryland, where he lives. His latest book is a collection of poems entitled *Mata Hari: Eye of the Day* (Apprentice House, Loyola University).

Author of 4 books of poetry, Carol Coffee Reposa has received 3 Pushcart Prize nominations, along with 3 Fulbright-Hays Fellowships, and twice has made the short list for Texas Poet Laureate. She is also a winner of the 2015 San Antonio Public Library's Art & Letters Award.

Marilee Richards has had her poems widely published in journals including *The Southern Review, Rattle, The Sun, Tar River Poetry, Santa Clara Review,* and *Tulane Review.* Her book, *A Common Ancestor,* was published by Hip Pocket Press.

Stephen R. Roberts collects books, knives, geodes, gargoyles, poetic lariats, and various other objects of interest to enhance his basic perceptions of a chaotic planet that pays little attention to him, as far as he knows. His book, *Almost Music From Between Places,* is available from Chatter House Press.

Seven-time Pushcart Prize nominee Russell Rowland is widely published in small journals. Two chapbooks, *Train of All Cabooses* and *Mountain Blue,* are available from Finishing Line Press. After years of propriety, he welcomes this chance to display the wise ass side of his personality.

Yvette A. Schnoeker-Shorb's work has appeared in *Red River Review, Dark Matter: A Journal of Speculative Writing, Aji Magazine, Sierra Nevada Review, Caesura, Twisted Vine Literary Arts Journal,* and *ArLiJo.* She is a past Pushcart Prize nominee, a recent Best of the Net nominee, and co-founder of Native West Press.

Dustin Scott: "Thank you to my wife for being a constant reminder of how I can improve to make her life better. I live to serve you and love every second. May my writing only be a shadow of my effort to be a better man for my wife's enjoyment."

Jan Seale, the 2012 Texas Poet Laureate, is a resident of the Lower Rio Grande Valley of Texas. Her writings include 9 books of poetry, 2 of short fiction, and 3 of nonfiction. Her latest books are *The Parkinson Poems*, *Appearances*, and *Nature Nurture Neither*.

Allison Sharp is a high-school English teacher by day, independent scholar by night. In her work, the Abilene Christian University grad focuses on the ways women move in society and how others react to difference.

Jon Simmons's poetry was awarded an Academy of American Poets Prize at Emerson College, where he graduated with a BFA in writing, literature, and publishing. His writings have appeared or are forthcoming in *Digital Americana, Litro, Drunken Boat, Grey Sparrow Journal*, and *Snail Mail Review*. John currently resides in Boston.

Wendy Sloan's work has appeared in journals and in the anthologies *Poems for a Liminal Age* and *The Best of the Raintown Review*. She has been a finalist for the Nemerov Sonnet Award and nominated for a Pushcart Prize. Sloan's first collection will be published by Kelsay Books in 2016.

Loren Smith currently lives in Logan, Utah, above a large book and music store. While this arrangement may seem romantic to some, parking authorities have sucked all the joy out of it. Consequently, he has committed himself to rediscovering bicycles and the thinning nature of walking.

Tyler Stoddard Smith's writing has been featured in: *UTNE Reader, McSweeney's, Esquire, The Best American Fantasy*, and *The Morning News*, among others. His book, *Whore Stories: A Revealing History of the World's Oldest Profession*, was named to Kirkus Reviews' Best of 2012.

Janice D. Soderling has poetry, fiction, essays and translations in print and online sites worldwide, in 8 anthologies and the UK teaching aid "Spotlight on Literacy: Creative Interventions." She's been a featured or invited reader at European and U.S. venues. Her numerous nominations and awards include *Glimmer Train Stories'* first prize.

Howard F. Stein, a poet as well as an applied, psychoanalytic, medical, humanistic, and organizational anthropologist, has published 28 books. He is professor emeritus in the department of family and preventive medicine, University of Oklahoma Health Sciences Center, Oklahoma City. He greatly admires Groucho Marx, an exemplary wise ass.

Bradley R. Strahan taught poetry at Georgetown University for 12 years. He has 6 poetry books and over 600 poems published worldwide. His 2011 book, *This Art of Losing*, was translated into French. A poetry book from a recent stay in Ireland was published by BrickHouse Books in late 2014.

Jeffrey Talmadge is a graduate of Duke University, the Warren Wilson MFA Program for Writers, and the University of Texas School of Law. His work has appeared in *The Texas Quarterly, The Greensboro Review, The Atlanta Review, Alabama Literary Review, Gargoyle*, and *The Hiram Poetry Review*. He lives in Georgia.

Larry D. Thomas, a member of the Texas Institute of Letters and the 2008 Texas Poet Laureate, has published several collections of poetry. His most recent collection is *As If Light Actually Matters: New & Selected Poems* (Texas Review Press).

Jeffrey Thomson is a poet, memoirist, and translator and is the author of multiple books including *fragile, Birdwatching in Wartime, The Complete Poems of Catullus*, and *From the Fishouse*. He has been an NEA Fellow and a Fulbright Distinguished Scholar. He is a professor at the University of Maine Farmington.

David Vancil is retired from the library at Indiana State University. His 4 poetry collections are *The Art School Baby, The Homesick Patrol, Night Photo*, and *Moon Walking*. Recent work appears in *Blue Unicorn* and *Concho River Review*. He is married with a daughter in college.

David Joez Villaverde is an alumnus of the University of Michigan. His writing has been featured in the *Belle Rêve Literary Journal, The Jewish Literary Journal, Restless, Runaway Hotel, Apocrypha and Abstractions, The Pittsburgh City Paper, Uppagus*, and the *Loyalhanna Review*. His writing can occasionally be found at schadenfreudeanslip.com.

Jason Walker holds an M.A. in English from the University of Alabama at Birmingham, where he currently teaches composition. His poems and

fictions have been published in *Measure, Cellpoems, Monkeybicycle*, and others. His reviews appear in *Birmingham Poetry Review*.

Will Wells is a college English professor. *Unsettled Accounts* (Ohio University/Swallow Press, 2010) won the Hollis Summers Poetry Prize. He has poems in *Image, Birmingham Poetry Review, River Styx, Comstock Review, Potomac Review, Evansville Review, Alabama Literary Review, The Cape Rock, Southwest Review*, and *32 poems*.

Tom Whalen's books include *Winter Coat* (poetry), *Dolls* (prose poems), and *The President in Her Towers* (novel). His translation of *Girlfriends, Ghosts, and Other Stories* by Robert Walser was published by *New York Review Books*. He teaches film studies at the State Academy of Art and Design in Stuttgart, Germany. See www.tomwhalen.com.

Harold Whit Williams is guitarist for the rock band Cotton Mather. He is recipient of the 2014 Mississippi Review Poetry Prize, and his collection *Backmasking* won the 2013 Robert Phillips Poetry Chapbook Prize from Texas Review Press. His latest collection, *Lost in the Telling*, is available from FutureCycle Press.

Robert Wood is mostly a closet poet, having retired from almost 50 years as a law professor and corporate lawyer. He has only recently submitted poems for publication with a satisfactorily low rate of rejection.

R. Scott Yarbrough's work has appeared in *The American Poetry Review, The Hollins Critic, Puerto Del Sol, Descant*, and *The Nassau Review*. An honored Texas Piper Professor of Literature, he is the author of *A Sort of Adam Infant Dropped: True Myths* (Ink Brush Press).

Kevin Zepper teaches at Minnesota State University Moorhead. He is the author of 4 chapbooks. Terrie Manno and Zepper are the music/poetry performing duo Lines&Notes. If reincarnated, Zepper would come back as a poisonous Brazilian frog or food author Anthony Bourdain.

Bob Ziller is an artist, poet, translator, curator, and singer. He is the author of *Van Gogh Surfing* and translator of Jean-Joseph Rabearivelo's *Translated from the Night* and *Almost Dreams*. His bands Bingo Quixote and Media Circus Extravaganza have been praised as "F***in' Brilliant" by Promoter 3, United Kingdom.

Richard Lee Zuras is the author of 2 novels: *The Honeymoon Corruption* and *The Bastard Year*, available on Amazon. Rich has published poems in *Confrontation, Red Rock Review, Poetry Nook, Jabberwock Review*, and *South Dakota Review*. He is Professor of Creative Writing at the University of Maine at Presque Isle.

The Wise Ass contest winners
        $750   Lyman Grant   Austin, TX
        $500   Barbara Astor   Bellbrook, OH
        $250   Tom Whalen   Stuttgart, Germany